BEATING INFLATION WITH REAL ESTATE

Expert Guidance

for

Wealth Building

KING SMARTY

Table Of Content

CHAPTER 1: Introduction.................... 3
Chapter 2: Understanding the Real Estate Market.. 11
Chapter 3: Building Wealth Through Real Estate.. 86
Chapter 4: Advantages of Real Estate Investments..141
Chapter 5: Overcoming Challenges in Real Estate Investment............................165
Chapter 6: Conclusion......................... 198
Chapter 7: Additional Resources......... 217

Protected by copyright law. No piece of this distribution might be repeated, disseminated, or communicated in any structure or using any and all means, including copying, recording, or other electronic or mechanical techniques, without the earlier written authorization of the distributer, with the exception of brief citations encapsulated in basic audits and certain other noncommercial purposes allowed by intellectual property regulation.

Copyright @ King Smarty, 2024.

CHAPTER 1

Introduction

A. The Impact of Inflation on Investments

Inflation is a significant economic phenomenon that affects the purchasing power of currency over time. When inflation occurs, the cost of goods and services increases, leading to a decrease in the value of money. This erosion of purchasing power has a profound impact on investments, as the returns generated may not keep pace with the rising costs of living.

1. **Understanding Inflation**:
Inflation is often measured by the Consumer Price Index (CPI), which tracks the average change in prices of a basket of

goods and services over time. Central banks aim to maintain a target inflation rate to promote economic stability, typically around 2-3% annually. However, inflation rates can vary widely depending on factors such as economic conditions, government policies, and external shocks.

2. **Effects on Investment Returns**:
Inflation erodes the real value of investment returns, reducing the purchasing power of future income streams. For example, if an investment generates a 5% return in a year with 3% inflation, the real return is only 2%. This means that investors need to earn returns above the inflation rate to preserve their wealth and maintain their standard of living.

3. **Impact on Asset Prices**:
Inflation can also influence asset prices, including stocks, bonds, and real estate. As the cost of living rises, investors may demand higher returns from financial assets

to compensate for the loss of purchasing power. Additionally, tangible assets like real estate can serve as a hedge against inflation, as their value tends to appreciate over time in response to rising prices.

4. **Challenges for Fixed-Income Investments**:

Fixed-income investments, such as bonds and savings accounts, are particularly vulnerable to inflationary pressures. The fixed interest payments they provide may not keep pace with inflation, leading to a decrease in real returns. This can erode the value of retirement savings and other income-generating assets.

5. **Importance of Inflation Protection**:

Given the long-term impact of inflation on investment returns, investors need to incorporate inflation protection strategies into their portfolio management. Real assets, such as real estate and commodities, can provide a hedge against inflation by preserving purchasing power and generating positive real returns over time.

By understanding the impact of inflation on investments, investors can make informed decisions to protect their wealth and achieve their financial goals in an uncertain economic environment. In the following sections, we will explore how real estate can serve as an effective hedge against inflation and provide expert guidance for wealth building in the face of rising prices.

B. Why Real Estate is a Hedge Against Inflation

Real estate has long been recognized as a reliable hedge against inflation due to several inherent characteristics that make it resistant to the erosive effects of rising prices. Understanding why real estate serves as an effective inflation hedge can provide valuable insights for investors seeking to preserve and grow their wealth over time.

1. **Tangible Asset Value**:
Unlike financial assets such as stocks and bonds, real estate is a tangible asset with intrinsic value derived from its physical structure and land. The value of real estate tends to appreciate over time, driven by factors such as population growth, urbanization, and improvements in infrastructure. As a result, real estate investments have historically demonstrated resilience in preserving purchasing power during periods of inflation.

2. Income Generation Potential:

Real estate investments offer the potential for stable and predictable income streams in the form of rental income. Inflationary pressures can lead to increases in rental rates over time, allowing investors to maintain or even enhance their cash flow streams. Additionally, real estate leases may include provisions for annual rent escalations tied to inflation indexes, providing further protection against rising prices.

3. Hard Asset Protection:

Real estate is a hard asset that provides tangible benefits beyond financial returns, such as shelter, commercial space, or agricultural production. These intrinsic qualities make real estate investments less susceptible to market volatility and inflationary pressures compared to purely financial assets. Moreover, real estate assets can be leveraged to generate additional income or appreciation potential through active management and development strategies.

4. **Inflation-linked Financing**:

Real estate investors can take advantage of inflation-linked financing options, such as long-term fixed-rate mortgages. In an inflationary environment, the real value of debt decreases over time as inflation erodes the purchasing power of money. This means that borrowers can effectively repay their mortgage obligations with less valuable currency, while retaining ownership of appreciating real estate assets. Additionally, inflation-linked financing can provide investors with leverage to amplify returns and hedge against inflation risks.

5. **Diversification Benefits**:

Including real estate investments in a diversified portfolio can enhance overall risk-adjusted returns and mitigate the impact of inflation on investment performance. Real estate exhibits low correlation with traditional financial assets, such as stocks and bonds, making it an attractive diversification tool for investors seeking to reduce portfolio volatility and preserve wealth over the long term.

By recognizing the unique attributes of real estate as an inflation hedge, investors can strategically allocate their capital to capitalize on the wealth preservation and growth opportunities offered by this asset class. In the following sections, we will delve deeper into the various strategies and considerations for leveraging real estate investments to beat inflation and achieve financial success.

Chapter 2

Understanding the Real Estate Market

A. Overview of the Real Estate Sector

The real estate sector encompasses a wide range of activities related to the acquisition, development, management, and utilization of land, properties, and physical assets. It is a multifaceted industry that plays a crucial role in the economy, driving economic growth, job creation, and wealth generation. Here's an overview of key components and dynamics within the real estate sector:

1. **Property Types**:
    Residential Real Estate: Includes single-family homes, condominiums, townhouses, apartments, and vacation properties primarily used for residential purposes.

Commercial Real Estate: Encompasses office buildings, retail centers, shopping malls, industrial warehouses, hotels, and mixed-use developments intended for commercial activities and business operations.

Industrial Real Estate: Includes manufacturing facilities, distribution centers, logistics parks, and warehouses used for industrial production, storage, and distribution activities.

Land Development: Involves the acquisition, entitlement, and development of raw land for residential, commercial, industrial, or mixed-use purposes, including land subdivision, site preparation, and infrastructure development.

2. **Market Segments**:

Primary Market: Major urban centers, metropolitan areas, and prime locations with high demand, liquidity, and property values, attracting institutional investors, developers, and multinational corporations.

Secondary Market: Secondary cities, suburban areas, and emerging markets with growth potential, offering investment opportunities, development prospects, and affordable properties outside primary markets.

Tertiary Market: Rural areas, small towns, and niche markets with limited demand, lower liquidity, and specialized property types, catering to local investors, lifestyle buyers, and niche market segments.

3. **Investment Strategies**:

Buy and Hold: Long-term investment strategy focused on acquiring income-producing properties, generating rental income, and building equity through property appreciation over time.

Fix and Flip: Short-term investment strategy involving the acquisition, renovation, and resale of distressed properties for profit, capitalizing on property value appreciation and market inefficiencies.

Development: Involves the acquisition, entitlement, construction, and sale or lease of new properties or development projects, including residential subdivisions, commercial developments, and mixed-use complexes.

Value-Add: Strategy focused on acquiring underperforming or undervalued properties, implementing strategic improvements, and repositioning assets to enhance value, increase rental income, and maximize returns.

4. **Market Dynamics**:

Supply and Demand: Fluctuations in property supply and demand dynamics influence market conditions, vacancy rates, rental levels, and property values, shaping investment opportunities and market trends.

Economic Indicators: Macroeconomic factors, such as GDP growth, employment levels, interest rates, inflation, and consumer confidence, impact real estate market fundamentals, investment returns, and investor sentiment.

Regulatory Environment: Government policies, zoning regulations, land use restrictions, and tax incentives influence property development, investment incentives, and market outcomes, requiring investors to navigate regulatory risks and compliance challenges.

5. **Professional Services**:

Real Estate Brokerage: Facilitates property transactions, leasing agreements, and sales negotiations between buyers, sellers, landlords, and tenants, providing market expertise, industry insights, and transactional support.

Property Management: Manages day-to-day operations, tenant relations, maintenance activities, and financial performance for real estate assets, ensuring property optimization, tenant satisfaction, and investment objectives.

Development and Construction: Oversees the planning, design, permitting, construction, and project management of real estate developments, coordinating with architects, engineers, contractors, and regulatory authorities to deliver projects on time and within budget.

The real estate sector is dynamic, diverse, and interconnected, encompassing a wide range of activities, participants, and market dynamics. Whether as an investor, developer, landlord, tenant, or service provider, understanding the complexities and opportunities within the real estate sector is essential for navigating market conditions, making informed decisions, and achieving success in real estate investments.

B. Types of Real Estate Investments

1. Residential Properties

Residential properties are one of the most common and accessible forms of real estate investment, encompassing a wide range of housing options from single-family homes to multi-unit apartment buildings. Understanding the dynamics of residential real estate investing is essential for individuals looking to build wealth through rental income, property appreciation, or homeownership.

a. **Single-Family Homes**:

Single-family homes are standalone properties designed to accommodate one family or household. Investors can purchase single-family homes as rental properties to generate passive income through tenant rent payments. These properties offer benefits such as ease of management, lower vacancy risks, and potential for capital appreciation in desirable neighborhoods.

b. **Multi-Family Properties**:

Multi-family properties consist of two or more residential units within a single building or complex. Examples include duplexes, triplexes, and apartment buildings. Investing in multi-family properties allows investors to leverage economies of scale, diversify rental income streams, and maximize cash flow potential. However, managing multi-family properties may require more time, resources, and expertise compared to single-family homes.

c. **Condominiums (Condos)**:

Condominiums are individual units within a larger residential complex or community, typically governed by a homeowners' association (HOA). Condo ownership provides investors with access to shared amenities and facilities, such as swimming pools, fitness centers, and security services. Condos offer a low-maintenance lifestyle and potential for appreciation, but investors should consider HOA fees and regulations when evaluating investment opportunities.

d. **Townhouses**: Townhouses are attached or semi-detached dwellings that share walls with neighboring units. These properties offer a balance between single-family homes and condos, combining the privacy of a standalone residence with the convenience of shared amenities and maintenance services. Townhouses are popular among first-time homebuyers and investors seeking affordable housing options in urban or suburban areas.

e. **Vacation Rental Properties**: Vacation rental properties, also known as short-term rentals or Airbnb properties, cater to tourists and travelers seeking temporary accommodation. Investors can generate rental income by leasing out their properties on a nightly or weekly basis, often at higher rates compared to long-term rentals. However, managing vacation rental properties requires careful marketing, maintenance, and guest management to ensure profitability and positive guest experiences.

Understanding the nuances of residential real estate investments, including property types, rental strategies, market trends, and regulatory considerations, is crucial for success in this segment of the real estate market. By conducting thorough due diligence, analyzing investment metrics, and aligning investment goals with risk tolerance, investors can capitalize on the wealth-building opportunities offered by residential properties.

2. Commercial Properties

Commercial properties encompass a diverse range of real estate assets used for business, retail, office, industrial, and hospitality purposes. Investing in commercial properties offers distinct advantages and challenges compared to residential real estate, requiring investors to understand the unique dynamics of each property type and market segment.

a. **Office Buildings**:
   Office buildings are commercial properties designed to accommodate businesses, professional services, and corporate tenants. These properties range from small office complexes to high-rise skyscrapers located in central business districts (CBDs) or suburban office parks. Investing in office buildings can provide stable rental income, long-term leases, and potential for capital appreciation based on tenant demand and market conditions.

b. **Retail Centers**:

Retail centers include shopping malls, strip malls, and neighborhood retail centers that house various retail stores, restaurants, and entertainment venues. Retail properties cater to consumer needs and preferences, offering convenience, accessibility, and a diverse mix of tenants. Retail investments can generate rental income through base rents, percentage-of-sales leases, and common area maintenance (CAM) charges, with potential for value-add opportunities through repositioning or redevelopment projects.

c. **Industrial Properties**:

Industrial properties comprise warehouses, distribution centers, manufacturing facilities, and logistics hubs used for storage, production, and distribution of goods. Industrial real estate benefits from growing e-commerce trends, increased demand for last-mile delivery services, and global supply chain dynamics. Investing in industrial properties can provide stable cash flow, long-term tenant relationships, and potential for portfolio diversification in the commercial real estate sector.

d. **Hospitality Properties**:

Hospitality properties include hotels, resorts, motels, and vacation rental properties catering to travelers and tourists. Hospitality investments offer revenue streams from room rentals, food and beverage services, event hosting, and ancillary amenities. Investors in hospitality properties should consider factors such as location, market demand, brand affiliation, and operational efficiency to maximize occupancy rates, average daily rates (ADR), and revenue per available room (RevPAR).

e. **Mixed-Use Developments**:

Mixed-use developments combine residential, commercial, and retail components within a single property or complex, creating vibrant live-work-play environments. These projects integrate various uses, such as residential apartments, office spaces, retail shops, restaurants, and recreational amenities, to meet the diverse needs of residents and tenants. Investing in mixed-use developments offers opportunities for synergies, value creation, and community-building, but requires careful planning, zoning approvals, and management oversight.

Commercial real estate investments require thorough market analysis, due diligence, and risk management to identify attractive opportunities, assess tenant creditworthiness, and optimize property performance. By understanding the specific characteristics, demands, and challenges of commercial properties, investors can leverage their expertise to generate consistent cash flow, enhance asset value, and achieve long-term financial success in the commercial real estate sector.

3. Land Acquisition

Land acquisition involves the purchase or acquisition of undeveloped land or vacant parcels for various purposes, including development, investment, conservation, or speculation. Investing in land offers unique opportunities and challenges, requiring investors to assess factors such as location, zoning regulations, land use restrictions, and potential for value appreciation.

a. **Development Opportunities**:

Land acquisition presents developers with opportunities to undertake new construction projects, including residential subdivisions, commercial developments, industrial parks, and mixed-use projects. Developers typically purchase land with the intention of obtaining necessary approvals, permits, and entitlements to commence construction and create value through development activities. Land acquisition strategies may involve identifying underutilized or distressed properties, negotiating favorable purchase terms, and conducting feasibility studies to assess project viability.

b. Investment Potential:

Land acquisition can serve as a strategic investment vehicle for individuals, institutions, and real estate investment funds seeking to capitalize on land appreciation and market growth. Investors may acquire land in high-growth areas, urban infill locations, or emerging markets with favorable demographics, infrastructure, and economic fundamentals. Land investments offer potential for long-term capital appreciation, portfolio diversification, and preservation of wealth against inflationary pressures.

c. **Conservation and Preservation**:

Land acquisition plays a critical role in environmental conservation, habitat preservation, and land stewardship efforts aimed at protecting natural resources, wildlife habitats, and scenic landscapes. Conservation-minded investors, nonprofit organizations, and government agencies may acquire land for conservation easements, wildlife refuges, public parks, or recreational use. Land conservation initiatives contribute to biodiversity conservation, climate resilience, and sustainable land management practices.

d. **Speculative Ventures**:

Land acquisition can also attract speculative investors seeking short-term gains or land banking opportunities. Speculative land investments involve purchasing land based on potential future value appreciation, rezoning opportunities, or anticipated changes in market conditions. Speculative land ventures carry higher risks due to uncertainties related to zoning approvals, regulatory changes, market volatility, and development timelines.

e. **Due Diligence and Risk Mitigation**: Successful land acquisition requires rigorous due diligence, including site inspections, environmental assessments, title searches, and legal reviews. Investors should evaluate factors such as soil conditions, topography, access to utilities, market demand, competition, and exit strategies when assessing land investment opportunities. Risk mitigation strategies may include diversification, financial analysis, contingency planning, and consulting with legal, financial, and real estate professionals.

Land acquisition offers investors a wide range of opportunities to create value, achieve financial goals, and contribute to sustainable land development. Whether pursuing development projects, long-term investments, conservation initiatives, or speculative ventures, investors should conduct thorough research, analysis, and

Beating Inflation with Real Estate

risk management to make informed decisions and maximize returns in the dynamic land marke

t.

4. REITs (Real Estate Investment Trusts) a.k.a buy-back investment

Real Estate Investment Trusts (REITs) are investment vehicles that allow individuals to invest in real estate assets without directly owning physical properties. REITs pool funds from multiple investors to invest in a diversified portfolio of income-generating properties, including residential, commercial, industrial, and hospitality assets. Investing in REITs offers several advantages, including liquidity, diversification, income generation, and potential for capital appreciation.

a. **Structure and Regulation**:

REITs are structured as publicly traded companies, private funds, or trusts that own and operate income-producing properties. To qualify as a REIT, a company must meet certain regulatory requirements, including distributing a significant portion of its taxable income to shareholders as dividends, investing primarily in real estate assets, and adhering to specific ownership and operational criteria. REITs are subject to oversight by regulatory bodies such as the Securities and Exchange Commission (SEC) in the United States.

b. **Types of REITs**:

REITs can be categorized based on their investment focus, property types, and operating structures. Common types of REITs include:

  - Equity REITs: Invest in and own income-producing real estate properties, generating revenue primarily from property rents and capital appreciation.

  - Mortgage REITs (mREITs): Invest in mortgage-backed securities, loans, and other debt instruments secured by real estate properties, earning income from interest payments and loan servicing fees.

  - Hybrid REITs: Combine elements of both equity and mortgage REITs, investing in a diversified portfolio of real estate properties and real estate-related debt instruments.

- Publicly Traded vs. Non-Traded REITs: Publicly traded REITs are listed on stock exchanges and trade like stocks, offering liquidity and transparency to investors. Non-traded REITs are not traded on public exchanges and may have limited liquidity, longer holding periods, and higher fees.

c. **Income Generation**:

REITs are required to distribute a significant portion of their taxable income to shareholders in the form of dividends, typically ranging from 90% to 100% of taxable income. As a result, REITs offer attractive dividend yields and consistent income streams, making them popular among income-oriented investors seeking passive cash flow and portfolio diversification.

d. **Capital Appreciation**:

In addition to dividend income, REITs can generate returns through capital appreciation of underlying real estate assets. Changes in property values, rental rates, occupancy levels, and market conditions can impact the value of REIT shares over time. Investors may benefit from potential appreciation in REIT share prices, especially in favorable economic environments and real estate markets.

e. **Risk Considerations**:

While REITs offer numerous benefits, they also carry certain risks that investors should be aware of, including:

- Market Risk: REIT share prices may fluctuate in response to changes in interest rates, economic conditions, industry trends, and investor sentiment.

- Property Risk: REITs are exposed to risks associated with property ownership, including vacancies, lease expirations, tenant defaults, property damage, and market obsolescence.

- Regulatory Risk: Changes in tax laws, regulations, and accounting standards can impact REITs' operational and financial performance, as well as their ability to qualify for tax-advantaged status.

Investing in REITs can provide investors with exposure to real estate markets, income-producing assets, and portfolio diversification benefits without the challenges of direct property ownership. By understanding the structure, types, income generation, capital appreciation potential, and risk considerations associated with REIT investments, investors can make informed decisions to achieve their financial goals and enhance their investment portfolios.

Are you ready to take your investments to the next level?

Let me show you how to earn up to 500k to 150,000,000 yearly as profit just by owning land.

This is called BUY BACK, a game-changing opportunity to grow your wealth through real estate.

HOW IT WORKS

First: Find a reputable Real Estate company such as Landview Property Investment Limited with a proven track record of business credibility.

Invest in a unit of land with a minimum of 1 Million Naira for a period of 6 months or 12 Months.

Resell to us at the end of your investment tenure with 25% profit after 6 Months or 50% profit after 12 Months.

✔ FLEXIBILITY & SECURITY

The following documents will be issued as legal documents to back up your investment

1. Receipt of Payment

2. Contract of Sale

3. A letter of Acknowledgment

4. A Post dated cheque to safeguard your funds and ensure a worry-free experience.

✔ EXPERT GUIDANCE

Our seasoned professionals will guide you every step of the way, providing personalized assistance and sharing valuable insights into the real estate market.

✔ CONSTANT GROWTH

Yes! You have the opportunity to take your profit and re-invest back into the scheme or you can decide to re-invest all back into the scheme. The more you invest the more money you make.

FOR EXAMPLE
Buy 1 plot for 1,000,000
Sell in 6 months for 1,250,000
Sell in 12 months for 1,500,000

Beating Inflation with Real Estate

BUY BACK PLAN

Earn up to 50% Profit

Invest	6 MONTHS 25% profit	10 MONTHS 40% profit	12 MONTHS 50% profit
₦1,000,000	₦1,250,000	₦1,400,000	₦1,500,000
₦2,000,000	₦2,500,000	₦2,800,000	₦3,000,000
₦3,000,000	₦3,750,000	₦4,200,000	₦4,500,000
₦4,000,000	₦5,000,000	₦5,600,000	₦6,000,000
₦5,000,000	₦6,250,000	₦7,000,000	₦7,500,000
₦6,000,000	₦7,500,000	₦8,400,000	₦9,000,000
₦7,000,000	₦8,750,000	₦9,800,000	₦10,500,000
₦8,000,000	₦10,000,000	₦11,200,000	₦12,000,000
₦9,000,000	₦11,250,000	₦12,600,000	₦13,500,000
₦10,000,000	₦12,500,000	₦14,000,000	₦15,000,000

To know more about this juicy investment offer, Message AMW PROPERTIES on WhatsApp. https://wa.me/2347061092227.

C. Explaining Real Estate Terminologies

1. Off-plan Projects

Off-plan projects, also known as pre-construction or pre-selling projects, refer to real estate developments that are sold before construction has commenced or completed. In off-plan projects, developers typically offer units or properties for sale based on architectural plans, designs, and project specifications, with the promise of delivering completed units at a future date.

a. **Reservation and Sales Process**:
In off-plan projects, developers typically launch sales campaigns to market and sell units to prospective buyers. Interested buyers are given the opportunity to reserve units by paying a reservation fee or deposit, which secures their position in the purchase

queue. Once reservations are confirmed, buyers may enter into purchase agreements or contracts with developers, outlining terms, conditions, and payment schedules for the purchase of off-plan properties.

b. **Advantages for Buyers**:

Off-plan projects offer several advantages for buyers, including:

- Potential for Early Access: Buyers can secure units at pre-construction prices and have the opportunity to choose preferred locations, floor plans, and finishes before construction begins.

- Price Appreciation: Off-plan properties may appreciate in value during the construction period and upon completion, allowing buyers to benefit from capital appreciation and potential resale profits.

- Payment Flexibility: Developers often offer flexible payment plans, installment options, and financing arrangements to facilitate off-plan purchases, making it accessible to a wider range of buyers.

- Investment Potential: Off-plan properties can serve as investment vehicles for capital growth, rental income, and portfolio diversification, offering potential returns over the long term.

c. **Risks and Considerations**:

Despite the potential benefits, off-plan projects entail certain risks and considerations for buyers, including:

- Construction Delays: Off-plan projects may face delays due to construction challenges, permitting issues, financing constraints, or unforeseen circumstances, leading to extended completion timelines and potential inconvenience for buyers.

- Developer Reputation: Buyers should conduct due diligence on developers' track record, financial stability, and project delivery capabilities to assess the reliability and credibility of off-plan projects.

- Market Fluctuations: Off-plan purchases are subject to market dynamics, economic conditions, and demand-supply trends, which can impact property values, rental yields, and resale prospects over time.

- Legal Protections: Buyers should review and understand the terms and conditions of off-plan purchase agreements, including provisions for refunds, warranties, dispute resolution, and regulatory compliance.

Off-plan projects offer buyers the opportunity to invest in real estate developments at early stages, potentially benefiting from price appreciation, customization options, and investment returns. However, buyers should carefully evaluate risks, conduct thorough research, and seek professional advice to make informed decisions and mitigate potential challenges associated with off-plan purchases.

2. Delivery Issues and Solutions

Delivery issues in real estate refer to challenges or delays in the completion and handover of properties to buyers or tenants as per the agreed-upon timelines. These issues can arise due to various factors, including construction delays, regulatory approvals, financing constraints, legal disputes, and unforeseen circumstances. Addressing delivery issues effectively requires proactive measures, communication, and collaboration among developers, contractors, regulatory authorities, and buyers or tenants.

a. **Common Delivery Issues**:
Delivery issues in real estate projects may include:
   - Construction Delays: Unforeseen construction challenges, material shortages, labor disputes, weather conditions, or logistical issues can lead to delays in project completion and occupancy.

- Regulatory Approvals: Delays in obtaining necessary permits, licenses, clearances, and approvals from government agencies can hinder construction progress and delay project delivery.
- Financing Constraints: Funding shortages, cost overruns, budgetary constraints, or liquidity issues can impede developers' ability to complete projects on schedule and meet contractual obligations.
- Legal Disputes: Litigation, arbitration, or disputes with contractors, suppliers, buyers, or regulatory authorities can disrupt project timelines and result in protracted delays or injunctions.
- Market Conditions: Economic downturns, market volatility, changes in consumer preferences, or shifts in demand-supply dynamics can affect developers' ability to sell or lease properties and generate revenue for project completion.

b. **Solutions to Address Delivery Issues**:

Developers and stakeholders can implement various strategies and solutions to mitigate delivery issues and ensure timely project completion, including:

- Project Management: Adopting effective project management practices, scheduling tools, and construction methodologies to streamline workflows, optimize resource allocation, and minimize delays.

- Risk Management: Conducting risk assessments, contingency planning, and scenario analysis to identify potential threats, mitigate project risks, and implement risk mitigation measures.

- Communication and Transparency: Maintaining open communication channels, regular updates, and transparent reporting with buyers, tenants, investors, and stakeholders to manage expectations, address concerns, and build trust.

- Collaboration and Coordination: Facilitating collaboration, coordination, and alignment among project teams, contractors, subcontractors, suppliers, consultants, and regulatory agencies to resolve issues and expedite approvals.

- Compliance and Governance: Adhering to regulatory requirements, building codes, environmental standards, and quality control measures to ensure compliance, minimize regulatory delays, and uphold project integrity.

- Financial Planning: Securing adequate financing, capital reserves, and contingency funds to address funding gaps, unforeseen costs, and financial challenges throughout the project lifecycle.

By proactively identifying, addressing, and mitigating delivery issues, developers and stakeholders can enhance project resilience, protect stakeholders' interests, and deliver successful real estate projects that meet quality standards, timelines, and expectations. Effective project management, risk mitigation, communication, collaboration, and financial planning are essential components of delivering real estate projects successfully amidst evolving market dynamics and challenges.

3. Evaluating Developers' Capacity and Reputation

Evaluating developers' capacity and reputation is crucial for investors, buyers, and stakeholders in the real estate industry to make informed decisions and mitigate risks associated with property development projects. Assessing developers' track record, financial strength, project management capabilities, and reputation in the market can help stakeholders determine the likelihood of successful project execution, timely delivery, and overall project quality.

a. **Track Record and Experience**:
 - Reviewing developers' past projects, completed developments, and portfolio of properties to assess their experience, expertise, and specialization in various real estate sectors, such as residential, commercial, industrial, and mixed-use developments.

- Analyzing developers' track record in terms of project delivery, construction quality, adherence to timelines and budgets, customer satisfaction, and compliance with regulatory requirements and industry standards.

- Seeking references, testimonials, and feedback from previous buyers, tenants, investors, industry professionals, and regulatory authorities to gauge developers' reputation, reliability, and performance in the market.

b. **Financial Strength and Stability**:

- Evaluating developers' financial standing, liquidity position, debt levels, cash flow, profitability, and ability to secure financing for new projects through equity, debt, or joint venture partnerships.

- Reviewing developers' balance sheets, income statements, cash flow statements, and financial ratios to assess their financial health, leverage ratios, solvency, and ability to withstand market downturns, economic shocks, or unforeseen challenges.

- Considering developers' credit ratings, creditworthiness, and relationships with financial institutions, lenders, investors, and stakeholders to determine their access to capital and ability to fund project developments.

c. **Project Management Capabilities**:

- Assessing developers' project management capabilities, organizational structure, leadership team, and talent pool of professionals, including architects, engineers, contractors, and project managers.

- Reviewing developers' project management processes, systems, and methodologies for planning, execution, monitoring, and control of development projects, including risk management, quality assurance, and stakeholder engagement.

- Examining developers' ability to navigate regulatory approvals, zoning requirements, permitting processes, environmental assessments, and community engagement initiatives to ensure compliance and minimize project delays.

d. **Reputation and Stakeholder Relations**:

- Investigating developers' reputation, brand image, and market positioning based on public perception, media coverage, industry awards, and recognition from peers, competitors, and stakeholders.
- Monitoring developers' relationships with buyers, tenants, homeowners' associations (HOAs), regulatory agencies, local communities, and other stakeholders to assess their commitment to ethical business practices, corporate social responsibility, and sustainable development.
- Conducting due diligence on developers' legal history, litigation records, regulatory

compliance, and ethical conduct to identify any past or pending legal issues, disputes, or controversies that may impact their reputation and credibility.

By evaluating developers' capacity and reputation through comprehensive due diligence, stakeholders can mitigate risks, build trust, and make informed decisions when investing in or partnering with developers on real estate projects. Transparent communication, collaboration, and alignment of interests between developers and stakeholders are essential for fostering long-term relationships and delivering successful real estate developments that create value for all parties involved.

4. Flipping Properties

Flipping properties, also known as property flipping or real estate flipping, is a real estate investment strategy where investors purchase properties with the intention of reselling them quickly for a profit. Flipping properties typically involves buying distressed or undervalued properties, renovating or improving them, and then selling them at a higher price to realize capital gains. This strategy requires careful planning, market analysis, renovation expertise, and effective execution to maximize returns and mitigate risks.

a. **Finding Opportunities**: Identifying distressed properties, foreclosure listings, bank-owned properties, short sales, estate sales, or motivated sellers who are willing to sell below market value due to financial hardship, foreclosure, divorce, relocation, or other reasons.

Conducting market research, property analysis, and comparative market analysis (CMA) to identify neighborhoods, locations, and property types with high demand, low inventory, and potential for value appreciation.

b. **Renovation and Improvement**:
Assessing the condition, structure, and potential of properties to determine renovation scope, budget, and timeline for improvements, repairs, and upgrades.

Hiring contractors, architects, designers, and other professionals to oversee renovation projects, obtain necessary permits, and ensure compliance with building codes, zoning regulations, and quality standards.

Implementing cost-effective renovation strategies, such as cosmetic updates, kitchen and bathroom remodels, flooring replacement, painting, landscaping, and curb appeal enhancements, to maximize property value and appeal to prospective buyers.

c. **Pricing and Marketing**:

Setting competitive listing prices, marketing strategies, and selling timelines based on market conditions, comparable sales, renovation costs, profit margins, and investor objectives.

Leveraging marketing channels, such as online listings, real estate websites, social media platforms, signage, open houses, and networking events, to showcase properties, attract buyers, and generate interest.

Working with real estate agents, brokers, investors, and wholesalers to facilitate property sales, negotiate offers, and expedite closing transactions.

d. **Risks and Considerations**:

Flipping properties involves inherent risks and challenges, including:

Market Fluctuations: Changes in market conditions, economic factors, interest rates, and consumer preferences can impact property values, demand, and sales timelines.

Renovation Costs: Unforeseen expenses, cost overruns, construction delays, and quality issues can affect renovation budgets and profit margins.

Financing Constraints: Securing financing for property acquisitions, renovations, and holding costs may require access to capital, creditworthiness, and favorable lending terms.

Legal and Regulatory Risks: Compliance with real estate laws, contracts, disclosures, and disclosure requirements is essential to avoid legal disputes, liabilities, and reputational damage.

- Competition: Flipping properties in competitive markets requires differentiation, market knowledge, and strategic positioning to attract buyers and outperform competitors.

e. **Exit Strategies**:

Flippers may pursue various exit strategies to realize profits from property sales, including wholesaling, assignments, fix-and-flip, buy-and-hold, lease options, seller financing, or joint venture partnerships, depending on market conditions and investor objectives.

Evaluating exit strategies based on factors such as market liquidity, capital requirements, holding periods, tax implications, and risk-return profiles to optimize returns and mitigate downside risks.

Successful property flipping requires a combination of market savvy, renovation expertise, financial acumen, and effective execution to identify, acquire, renovate, and sell properties profitably. By understanding the dynamics of property flipping, conducting thorough due diligence, and implementing sound investment strategies, investors can capitalize on opportunities in the real estate market and achieve their financial goals.

5. Title and Documentation

Title and documentation play a critical role in real estate transactions, providing legal proof of ownership, rights, and encumbrances associated with properties. Clear and marketable title, supported by accurate and comprehensive documentation, is essential for facilitating property transfers, securing financing, and mitigating risks for buyers, sellers, lenders, and other stakeholders involved in real estate transactions.

a. **Title Search and Examination**:
 - Conducting a title search and examination involves reviewing public records, land registries, and title documents to verify ownership history, property boundaries, easements, liens, encumbrances, and legal claims affecting the property.

Engaging title companies, attorneys, or title agents to perform due diligence, title searches, and title insurance underwriting to identify any defects, discrepancies, or title issues that may affect property ownership or marketability.

b. **Title Insurance**:
Title insurance policies protect buyers, lenders, and property owners against financial losses arising from defects, errors, or challenges to property titles, such as undisclosed liens, boundary disputes, forged deeds, or invalid conveyances.

Purchasing title insurance policies, such as owner's title insurance and lender's title insurance, provides coverage for title defects, legal challenges, and financial losses incurred due to title-related issues.

c. **Legal Documents and Contracts**:
Real estate transactions require various legal documents, contracts, and agreements to formalize property transfers, financing arrangements, and other contractual obligations between parties.

Common legal documents in real estate transactions include purchase agreements, sales contracts, deeds, mortgages, promissory notes, lease agreements, property disclosures, closing statements, and legal disclosures required by state and federal laws.

d. **Due Diligence and Disclosures**:

Buyers, sellers, and real estate professionals must conduct due diligence, disclose material facts, and provide accurate information about properties to ensure transparency, fairness, and compliance with legal and ethical standards.

Disclosures may include property condition reports, environmental assessments, hazard disclosures, lead paint disclosures, HOA disclosures, zoning restrictions, and other statutory disclosures required by law.

e. **Closing and Recording**:

The closing process involves finalizing real estate transactions, executing legal documents, disbursing funds, and transferring ownership rights from sellers to buyers.

Recording legal documents, such as deeds, mortgages, and liens, with county or municipal recording offices establishes public notice of property ownership, encumbrances, and other legal interests, providing protection for buyers and lenders against subsequent claims or challenges to property titles.

f. **Regulatory Compliance**:

Real estate transactions are subject to regulatory requirements, laws, and regulations at the federal, state, and local levels, governing property transfers, disclosures, consumer protections, fair housing practices, and environmental regulations.

Compliance with real estate laws, regulations, and regulatory agencies, such as the Consumer Financial Protection Bureau (CFPB), the Department of Housing and Urban Development (HUD), and state real estate commissions, is essential to ensure legal compliance and avoid penalties, fines, or legal liabilities.

Ensuring clear, marketable title and accurate documentation in real estate transactions is essential for protecting property rights, minimizing legal risks, and facilitating smooth and transparent transactions for all parties involved. Working with experienced real estate professionals, attorneys, title companies, and other experts can help buyers, sellers, and lenders navigate the complexities of title and documentation requirements in real estate transactions.

6. Land Banking

Land banking is a real estate investment strategy that involves acquiring and holding undeveloped land with the intention of profiting from future development, appreciation, or rezoning opportunities. Land banking investors purchase parcels of land in strategic locations, often on the outskirts of urban areas, growth corridors, or areas earmarked for future development, and hold onto them for extended periods until market conditions become favorable for development or resale.

a. **Long-Term Investment Horizon**:
Land banking typically involves a long-term investment horizon, as investors may hold land parcels for several years or even decades before realizing returns. This strategy requires patience, strategic planning, and the ability to withstand fluctuations in land values, market cycles, and economic conditions.

b. **Strategic Location Selection**:

Successful land banking relies on strategic location selection, where investors target land parcels in areas with high growth potential, infrastructure development, population expansion, and urbanization trends. Proximity to transportation hubs, major highways, employment centers, schools, and amenities can enhance the value and desirability of land parcels.

c. **Zoning and Development Potential**:

Investors assess the zoning regulations, land use designations, and development potential of land parcels to identify opportunities for rezoning, entitlements, or land use changes that could increase property values and unlock development opportunities. Engaging with local planning authorities, conducting feasibility studies, and understanding zoning ordinances are critical aspects of land banking.

d. **Passive Investment Strategy**:
Land banking is often considered a passive investment strategy, as investors hold onto land parcels without actively developing or improving them. Instead, investors focus on land acquisition, due diligence, land entitlements, and monitoring market conditions to capitalize on appreciation and development opportunities over time.

e. **Risk Mitigation and Diversification**:
Land banking offers potential risk mitigation and diversification benefits for investors seeking to hedge against market volatility, inflation, and economic downturns. Land investments may have lower carrying costs, minimal maintenance requirements, and lower liquidity compared to developed properties, making them attractive components of diversified investment portfolios.

f. **Market Timing and Exit Strategies**:

Timing is crucial in land banking, as investors must assess market conditions, land supply-demand dynamics, and economic indicators to determine the optimal time to enter, hold, or exit land investments. Exit strategies for land banking investments may include selling land parcels to developers, subdividing parcels for resale, or participating in joint ventures or partnerships for development projects.

g. **Due Diligence and Regulatory Compliance**:

Land banking investors conduct thorough due diligence, including title searches, land surveys, environmental assessments, and regulatory reviews, to assess the feasibility and risks associated with land acquisitions. Compliance with zoning regulations, environmental laws, and permitting requirements is essential to avoid legal and regulatory issues.

Land banking offers investors the potential for capital appreciation, passive income, and portfolio diversification through strategic acquisition and holding of undeveloped land parcels. By carefully selecting land parcels in high-growth areas, understanding zoning and development potential, and conducting thorough due diligence, investors can capitalize on land banking opportunities to generate long-term returns and preserve wealth over time.

7. Payment Structure (Outright and Installment)

The payment structure in real estate transactions refers to the terms, conditions, and arrangements for the purchase or acquisition of properties, including the timing, amount, and method of payment. Two common payment structures in real estate transactions are outright payment and installment payment, each offering distinct advantages and considerations for buyers, sellers, and investors.

a. **Outright Payment**:

Outright payment, also known as cash payment or lump-sum payment, involves the buyer paying the full purchase price of the property upfront at the time of closing or settlement.

Advantages:

Certainty and Convenience: Outright payment provides sellers with immediate liquidity and certainty of funds, simplifying the transaction process and reducing administrative burdens.

Negotiating Power: Buyers who can offer outright payment may have stronger negotiating leverage, as sellers may prefer cash offers due to their ability to close quickly and with minimal contingencies.

Avoidance of Interest Costs: Outright payment eliminates the need for financing, mortgage interest, and loan fees, saving buyers money on borrowing costs over the long term.

Considerations:

Liquidity Requirements: Outright payment requires buyers to have sufficient cash reserves, savings, or liquid assets to cover the full purchase price of the property, which may limit affordability for some buyers.

Opportunity Cost: Buyers who opt for outright payment may miss out on potential investment opportunities or alternative uses for their funds, such as diversifying investments, earning higher returns, or maintaining liquidity for emergencies.

b. **Installment Payment**:

Installment payment, also known as financing or deferred payment, involves buyers paying the purchase price of the property in multiple installments over a specified period, typically through a loan or financing arrangement.

Advantages:

Affordability: Installment payment allows buyers to spread the cost of purchasing the property over time, making homeownership more accessible and affordable for individuals who may not have the funds for outright payment.

Preserving Liquidity: Installment payment preserves buyers' liquidity and financial flexibility, allowing them to retain cash reserves for other purposes, such as emergencies, investments, or business opportunities.

Tax Benefits: Buyers who finance their purchases may be eligible for tax deductions on mortgage interest payments, property taxes, and other homeownership expenses, reducing their overall tax liability.

Considerations:

Interest Costs: Installment payment involves interest costs, loan origination fees, and other financing expenses, which increase the total cost of purchasing the property over the loan term.

Qualification Requirements: Buyers seeking installment payment options must meet lender requirements, including creditworthiness, income verification, debt-to-income ratios, and down payment obligations, which may limit eligibility for some buyers.

Long-Term Commitment: Installment payment requires buyers to commit to repaying the loan over an extended period, typically 15 to 30 years, which entails long-term financial obligations and responsibilities.

c. **Hybrid Payment Structures**:

Some real estate transactions may involve hybrid payment structures that combine elements of outright and installment payment, such as providing a portion of the purchase price upfront with the remainder paid in installments over time.

Hybrid payment structures offer flexibility and customization options for buyers and sellers, allowing them to negotiate terms, payment schedules, and financing arrangements that meet their specific needs, preferences, and financial circumstances.

Understanding the implications of outright and installment payment structures is essential for buyers, sellers, and investors to make informed decisions and navigate real estate transactions effectively. Whether opting for cash purchases or financing options, individuals should consider their financial goals, risk tolerance, cash flow needs, and long-term affordability when determining the most suitable payment structure for their real estate investments.

8. Promo Price and Pre-launch Price

Promo price and pre-launch price are marketing strategies used by real estate developers to attract buyers and investors to purchase properties during the initial stages of a development project. These pricing strategies offer buyers exclusive incentives, discounts, and promotional offers to encourage early commitment and investment in the project. Understanding the advantages of promo price and pre-launch price can help buyers capitalize on opportunities to secure properties at favorable terms and maximize potential returns.

a. **Promo Price**:

Promo price refers to discounted or incentivized pricing offered by developers for a limited time or promotional period to stimulate sales and generate buyer interest in a new development project.
Advantages:

Cost Savings: Promo price offers buyers the opportunity to purchase properties at reduced prices, saving money on the overall purchase price, closing costs, and financing expenses.

Value-Added Incentives: Promo price packages may include value-added incentives, such as waived application fees, closing cost assistance, free upgrades, furniture packages, or maintenance services, enhancing the value proposition for buyers.

Competitive Advantage: Buyers who take advantage of promo price offers may gain a competitive advantage over later buyers by securing preferred units, floor plans, or locations within the development at lower prices.

Immediate Equity: Purchasing properties at promo prices can result in immediate equity appreciation if market values increase over time, allowing buyers to build wealth and generate potential capital gains upon resale.

b. **Pre-launch Price**:

Pre-launch price refers to special pricing offered by developers to early investors or insiders before the official launch or public release of a development project.

Advantages:

Early Access: Pre-launch price offers buyers the opportunity to access exclusive pricing and inventory options before properties are widely marketed or available to the general public, allowing them to secure desirable units or locations.

Price Appreciation: Properties purchased at pre-launch prices may appreciate in value as the project progresses through construction, development, and completion stages, resulting in potential capital appreciation and investment returns for buyers.

First Mover Advantage: Pre-launch buyers may benefit from first-mover advantages, such as preferred pricing, priority selection, and insider access to project updates, information, and development progress.

Investment Opportunity: Pre-launch price presents an investment opportunity for buyers to capitalize on early-stage pricing discounts, leverage market demand, and participate in the growth potential of the development project from inception to completion.

c. **Actual Price**:

The actual price, also known as the market price or prevailing market value, refers to the price at which properties are sold or valued based on current market conditions, demand-supply dynamics, and comparable sales data.

Buyers who purchase properties at promo price or pre-launch price may realize significant cost savings or investment gains compared to the actual price when properties are sold or appraised at their full market value upon completion or resale.

Understanding the advantages of promo price and pre-launch price as the best time to buy property can help buyers make informed decisions and capitalize on opportunities to acquire properties at discounted prices, secure favorable terms, and maximize potential returns on their real estate investments. By leveraging exclusive pricing offers, incentives, and early access opportunities, buyers can gain a competitive edge in the market and achieve their financial goals with strategic property acquisitions.

9. Mortgage

A mortgage is a type of loan provided by financial institutions, such as banks, credit unions, or mortgage lenders, to enable individuals or businesses to purchase real estate properties by borrowing funds against the value of the property being purchased. Mortgages typically involve a borrower (mortgagor) obtaining financing from a lender (mortgagee) to acquire a property, with the property itself serving as collateral for the loan. Understanding how mortgages work, their types, terms, and considerations is essential for prospective homebuyers and real estate investors seeking to finance property acquisitions.

a. **Types of Mortgages**:

Fixed-Rate Mortgage: A fixed-rate mortgage offers a stable interest rate and monthly payment over the loan term, providing predictability and budgeting certainty for borrowers. Fixed-rate mortgages are available in various terms, such as 30-year, 20-year, or 15-year terms, with longer terms typically resulting in lower monthly payments but higher total interest costs over the loan term.

Adjustable-Rate Mortgage (ARM): An adjustable-rate mortgage features an interest rate that fluctuates periodically based on market conditions, economic indicators, or benchmark interest rates. ARMs typically offer lower initial interest rates and monthly payments during an introductory period, known as the initial fixed-rate period, followed by adjustments based on specified index rates and margins.

Government-Insured Mortgages: Government-sponsored entities, such as the Federal Housing Administration (FHA), Department of Veterans Affairs (VA), or the U.S. Department of Agriculture (USDA), offer mortgage programs that provide insurance or guarantees to lenders, reducing their risk and enabling borrowers to qualify for financing with lower down payments, credit score requirements, or income qualifications.

Jumbo Mortgages: Jumbo mortgages are loans that exceed the conforming loan limits set by government-sponsored enterprises, such as Fannie Mae and Freddie Mac. Jumbo mortgages are typically used for financing high-value properties that exceed conventional loan limits and may have stricter qualification criteria, higher interest rates, and larger down payment requirements.

Interest-Only Mortgage: An interest-only mortgage allows borrowers to make interest-only payments during an initial period, typically five to ten years, followed by fully amortizing payments for the remaining loan term. Interest-only mortgages offer lower initial payments but may result in higher payments after the interest-only period ends.

b. **Mortgage Terms and Components**:

Principal: The principal is the initial loan amount borrowed by the borrower to purchase the property. Repayments made by the borrower gradually reduce the principal balance over the loan term.

Interest Rate: The interest rate represents the cost of borrowing funds, expressed as an annual percentage rate (APR). Interest rates may be fixed or adjustable and can significantly impact the total cost of borrowing over the loan term.

Amortization: Amortization refers to the process of paying off the mortgage loan through regular installment payments, consisting of both principal and interest components, over the loan term.

Down Payment: The down payment is the initial cash payment made by the borrower towards the purchase price of the property. Down payment requirements vary by loan program and lender, with conventional mortgages typically requiring down payments ranging from 3% to 20% of the purchase price.

Loan Term: The loan term is the period over which the mortgage loan is repaid, typically ranging from 15 to 30 years for fixed-rate mortgages and 5 to 10 years for adjustable-rate mortgages. Shorter loan terms result in higher monthly payments but lower total interest costs over the loan term.

c. **Mortgage Process and Considerations**:

Prequalification: Prequalification involves assessing a borrower's financial situation, creditworthiness, and eligibility for mortgage financing based on preliminary information provided to the lender. Prequalification helps borrowers understand their purchasing power, loan options, and affordability before shopping for properties.

Preapproval: Preapproval involves obtaining a conditional loan approval from a lender based on a comprehensive review of the borrower's credit history, income, assets, and financial documentation. Preapproval strengthens a buyer's offer and demonstrates their readiness and ability to secure financing for a property purchase.

Loan Application: The mortgage application process involves completing a formal loan application, providing documentation, such as pay stubs, tax returns, bank statements, and employment verification, and undergoing underwriting review by the lender to evaluate the borrower's creditworthiness and risk profile.

Closing: The closing process, also known as settlement or escrow, involves finalizing the mortgage loan, executing legal documents, transferring ownership of the property, and disbursing funds to complete the transaction. Closing costs, including loan origination fees, appraisal fees, title insurance, and prepaid expenses, are typically paid by the buyer or seller at closing.

d. **Mortgage Benefits and Considerations**:

Homeownership: Mortgages enable individuals to achieve homeownership by providing access to financing for purchasing residential properties, building equity, and enjoying the benefits of homeownership, such as stability, privacy, and tax advantages.

Leverage: Mortgages allow buyers to leverage their investment by borrowing funds to purchase properties with a smaller initial cash outlay, enabling them to maximize returns and potentially achieve higher investment gains through property appreciation.

Tax Deductions: Mortgage interest payments and property taxes

Chapter 3

Building Wealth Through Real Estate

B. Strategies for Wealth Building

Building wealth through real estate involves employing strategic investment strategies, leveraging financial instruments, and maximizing the value of real estate assets to achieve long-term financial growth and prosperity. Various strategies can be employed to build wealth through real estate, including:

1. **Buy and Hold**:
The buy-and-hold strategy involves acquiring properties with the intention of holding them for an extended period, allowing them to appreciate in value over time while generating rental income. Investors focus on properties in

high-demand areas with strong fundamentals, such as job growth, population growth, and infrastructure development, to capitalize on long-term appreciation and cash flow potential.

2. **Value-Add Investing**:

Value-add investing entails purchasing properties that are underperforming, distressed, or in need of renovation or repositioning, making improvements to increase their value, and then either selling them for a profit or holding them for rental income. Value-add strategies may include property renovations, rebranding, tenant improvements, or rezoning to enhance property value and generate higher returns.

3. **Real Estate Development**:

Real estate development involves acquiring land or existing properties, obtaining entitlements, permits, and approvals, and constructing new developments, such as residential communities, commercial buildings, or mixed-use projects. Developers aim to create value by transforming underutilized or vacant land into income-producing assets that meet market demand and generate returns through sales or leasing.

4. **Passive Investments**:

Passive real estate investments, such as real estate investment trusts (REITs), real estate crowdfunding, or syndications, allow investors to pool their capital with other investors to invest in a diversified portfolio of properties without direct involvement in property management or operations. Passive investments offer liquidity, diversification, and professional management while providing exposure to real estate markets and income-producing assets.

5. **Leverage**:

Leveraging involves using borrowed funds, such as mortgage financing, to acquire properties with a smaller initial cash investment, thereby amplifying potential returns and increasing the purchasing power of investors. By leveraging OPM (Other People's Money), investors can control larger assets, magnify cash flow, and accelerate wealth accumulation through appreciation and equity growth.

6. **Tax Benefits**:

Real estate investments offer various tax advantages and incentives that can help investors reduce tax liabilities and increase after-tax returns. Tax benefits may include depreciation deductions, mortgage interest deductions, property tax deductions, 1031 exchanges, and capital gains tax deferral, allowing investors to optimize tax efficiency and preserve more of their investment gains.

7. **Portfolio Diversification**:

Real estate investments can serve as a diversification strategy within an investment portfolio, providing non-correlated returns, inflation protection, and a hedge against market volatility. By allocating a portion of their investment capital to real estate assets, investors can mitigate risks, enhance portfolio stability, and achieve a balanced asset allocation that aligns with their risk tolerance and investment objectives.

Implementing strategic wealth-building strategies in real estate requires careful planning, market analysis, risk management, and execution to capitalize on opportunities, mitigate risks, and achieve long-term financial success. By diversifying investment strategies, leveraging financial instruments, and optimizing tax advantages, investors can build wealth through real estate and create a sustainable path to financial independence and prosperity.

1. Long-term Property Investment

Long-term property investment involves acquiring real estate assets with the intention of holding them for an extended period, typically five years or more, to capitalize on appreciation, rental income, and wealth accumulation over time. This investment strategy focuses on building equity, generating passive income, and achieving long-term financial goals through strategic property acquisitions and portfolio management. Several key elements characterize long-term property investment:

a. **Wealth Accumulation**:

Long-term property investment aims to build wealth steadily over time by leveraging the power of compounding growth, capital appreciation, and income generation from rental properties. Investors seek to accumulate equity through property ownership, mortgage amortization, and value appreciation, resulting in increased net worth and asset appreciation over the investment horizon.

b. **Income Generation**:

Rental income from long-term property investments provides investors with a reliable source of passive income, supplementing other sources of revenue and supporting financial stability and independence. By leasing properties to tenants, investors can generate regular cash flow to cover mortgage payments, operating expenses, and provide a steady stream of income for living expenses or reinvestment.

c. **Portfolio Diversification**:

Long-term property investment offers diversification benefits within an investment portfolio, providing non-correlated returns, inflation protection, and a hedge against market volatility. Real estate assets have historically exhibited low correlation with traditional financial assets, such as stocks and bonds, making them an effective diversification tool for mitigating portfolio risks and enhancing long-term returns.

d. **Appreciation Potential**:

Property values tend to appreciate over the long term due to factors such as supply-demand dynamics, population growth, economic expansion, and inflationary pressures. Long-term property investors benefit from capital appreciation as property values increase over time, allowing them to realize substantial gains when selling properties or refinancing equity.

e. **Tax Advantages**:

Long-term property investment offers various tax benefits and incentives that can help investors reduce tax liabilities and increase after-tax returns. Tax advantages may include depreciation deductions, mortgage interest deductions, property tax deductions, capital gains tax deferral, and tax-free exchanges, allowing investors to optimize tax efficiency and preserve more of their investment gains.

f. **Risk Management**:

Long-term property investors employ risk management strategies to mitigate risks associated with real estate investments, such as market fluctuations, tenant turnover, vacancy risks, and unexpected expenses. Diversifying property holdings across different asset classes, geographic locations, and market segments can help spread risk and minimize exposure to specific market conditions or economic downturns.

g. **Strategic Planning**:

Successful long-term property investment requires strategic planning, market research, and financial analysis to identify investment opportunities, assess market trends, and evaluate property fundamentals. Investors conduct due diligence, feasibility studies, and risk assessments to make informed investment decisions and optimize portfolio performance over the investment horizon.

h. **Property Management**:

Effective property management is essential for long-term investment success, ensuring properties are well-maintained, leased to qualified tenants, and optimized for income generation and value appreciation. Investors may choose to self-manage properties or hire professional property management firms to oversee day-to-day operations, tenant relations, maintenance, and financial reporting.

Long-term property investment offers investors the potential for wealth accumulation, income generation, and portfolio diversification over time. By adopting a disciplined investment approach, leveraging market opportunities, and managing risks effectively, investors can build a sustainable real estate portfolio that aligns with their financial goals and objectives for long-term financial success.

3. Rental Income

Rental income is a key component of real estate investing, generating revenue through leasing properties to tenants in exchange for periodic rental payments. This income stream provides investors with a steady source of cash flow, passive income, and wealth accumulation potential, making rental properties an attractive investment option for both individual and institutional investors. Several key aspects characterize rental income and its role in real estate investment:

a. **Passive Income Generation**:

Rental income provides investors with a consistent source of passive income, allowing them to generate revenue without actively participating in day-to-day property management or operations. By leasing properties to tenants, investors can earn regular rental payments to cover mortgage expenses, operating costs, and generate surplus cash flow for living expenses or reinvestment.

b. **Diversification and Stability**:
Rental income offers diversification benefits within an investment portfolio, providing stable, predictable returns that are less susceptible to market fluctuations or economic volatility compared to other asset classes. Real estate assets have historically exhibited low correlation with traditional financial assets, such as stocks and bonds, making them a valuable diversification tool for mitigating portfolio risks and enhancing overall stability.

c. **Wealth Accumulation**:
Rental income plays a crucial role in wealth accumulation for real estate investors, enabling them to build equity, increase net worth, and achieve long-term financial goals through property ownership. Rental properties appreciate in value over time, allowing investors to benefit from

capital appreciation while generating passive income from rental operations.

d. Cash Flow Management:
Effective cash flow management is essential for maximizing rental income and optimizing property performance. Investors must carefully monitor rental expenses, such as mortgage payments, property taxes, insurance premiums, maintenance costs, and vacancy allowances, to ensure positive cash flow and profitability from rental operations.

e. Market Analysis and Rental Pricing:
Rental income depends on market demand, rental rates, and property characteristics, such as location, size, condition, and amenities. Investors conduct market analysis, comparative market studies, and rental surveys to determine optimal rental pricing, identify competitive rental rates, and position properties

effectively within the market to attract qualified tenants.

f. **Tenant Screening and Lease Management**:

Tenant selection and lease management are critical aspects of rental income generation, ensuring properties are leased to reliable, creditworthy tenants who adhere to lease terms and obligations. Investors screen prospective tenants, verify income and creditworthiness, and conduct background checks to minimize tenant turnover, rent arrears, and eviction risks.

g. **Property Maintenance and Upkeep**:

Maintaining rental properties in good condition is essential for attracting tenants, preserving property value, and maximizing rental income. Investors invest in property maintenance, repairs, and upgrades to enhance curb appeal, tenant satisfaction, and long-term asset value, thereby safeguarding rental income and optimizing property performance.

h. **Lease Negotiation and Renewal**:

Lease negotiation and renewal strategies can impact rental income and property profitability. Investors negotiate lease terms, rental concessions, and renewal options with tenants to optimize rental rates, minimize vacancy risks, and maximize rental income over the lease term. Lease renewals allow investors to retain existing tenants, avoid turnover costs, and maintain consistent cash flow from rental operations.

Rental income serves as a cornerstone of real estate investing, offering investors a reliable, recurring revenue stream, passive income, and wealth-building opportunities through property ownership and leasing activities. By effectively managing rental properties, optimizing rental pricing, and maintaining tenant relationships, investors can generate consistent cash flow, achieve financial independence, and build long-term wealth through real estate investments.

4. Real Estate Investment Trust (REIT) Investments

Real Estate Investment Trusts (REITs) are investment vehicles that enable individuals to invest in income-generating real estate properties without directly owning or managing the properties themselves. REITs pool capital from multiple investors to acquire, operate, and manage a diversified portfolio of real estate assets, including commercial properties, residential properties, industrial facilities, healthcare facilities, hotels, and infrastructure projects. Investing in REITs offers several advantages and considerations for investors:

a. **Diversification**:

REIT investments provide investors with exposure to a diversified portfolio of real estate assets across different property types, geographic regions, and market segments. By investing in REITs, investors can achieve portfolio diversification, mitigate concentration risks, and access a broad range of income-producing properties that may be otherwise inaccessible or cost-prohibitive to acquire individually.

b. **Passive Income**:

REITs generate income through rental revenue, property appreciation, and dividend distributions to shareholders. By investing in REITs, investors can earn passive income and regular dividend payments without the burden of property management, tenant relations, or day-to-day operations associated with direct real estate ownership. REIT dividends are typically higher than those of traditional stocks and bonds, making them an attractive income-generating investment option.

c. **Liquidity**:

REITs offer liquidity and tradability, allowing investors to buy and sell shares on public stock exchanges like any other publicly traded security. Unlike direct real estate investments, which may be illiquid and require time-consuming transactions to buy or sell properties, REIT shares can be bought or sold quickly and easily, providing investors with flexibility and access to capital when needed.

d. **Professional Management**:

REITs are managed by professional management teams, experienced real estate professionals, and property managers who oversee property acquisition, leasing, operations, and asset management activities on behalf of investors. By entrusting the management of real estate assets to professionals, investors benefit from expertise, economies of scale, and operational efficiencies that enhance property performance and investment returns.

e. **Tax Efficiency**:

REITs are required by law to distribute at least 90% of their taxable income to shareholders in the form of dividends, allowing them to qualify for favorable tax treatment. As pass-through entities, REIT dividends are taxed at the individual shareholder level, typically at lower dividend tax rates compared to ordinary income tax rates, providing investors with tax-efficient income and potential tax savings.

f. **Growth Potential**:

REIT investments offer growth potential through property appreciation, rental income growth, and strategic portfolio expansion. As real estate markets evolve and property values increase over time, REITs may realize capital appreciation and value enhancement opportunities that result in higher returns and increased shareholder wealth over the long term.

g. **Risk Considerations**:

While REIT investments offer diversification and income potential, they also entail certain risks, including market risks, interest rate risks, liquidity risks, and regulatory risks. Real estate markets are cyclical and sensitive to economic conditions, interest rate fluctuations, and market sentiment, which can impact property values, rental income, and REIT performance. Additionally, changes in tax laws, regulatory requirements, or industry dynamics may affect REIT operations and investment returns.

h. **Investment Selection**:

When investing in REITs, investors should conduct due diligence, research, and analysis to evaluate REITs' investment objectives, portfolio composition, financial performance, management quality, and dividend sustainability. Factors to consider include property types, geographic diversification, occupancy rates, lease terms, tenant credit quality, dividend history, expense ratios, and total return potential.

Overall, REIT investments offer investors an accessible and efficient way to participate in the real estate market, diversify their investment portfolios, and generate passive income through income-producing properties. By understanding the advantages, risks, and considerations associated with REIT investments, investors can make informed decisions and incorporate REITs into their investment strategies to achieve their financial goals and objectives.

B. Assessing Risks and Rewards

When it comes to real estate investments, understanding and evaluating the associated risks and rewards are essential for making informed decisions and achieving long-term financial success. Assessing risks and rewards involves analyzing various factors, market conditions, and investment considerations to determine the potential returns, challenges, and vulnerabilities of real estate investments. Here are key aspects to consider when assessing the risks and rewards of real estate investments:

1. **Market Risks**:

Market risks refer to factors that impact real estate markets, such as economic conditions, supply-demand dynamics, interest rates, demographic trends, and geopolitical events. Fluctuations in market conditions can affect property values, rental income, occupancy rates, and investment returns, making it crucial for investors to monitor market trends and anticipate potential risks.

2. **Property-Specific Risks**:

Property-specific risks pertain to factors related to individual properties, such as location, condition, occupancy, tenant quality, and lease terms. Properties located in high-demand areas with strong fundamentals, such as job growth, population growth, and infrastructure development, may have lower risks and higher potential returns compared to properties in declining or volatile markets.

3. **Financial Risks**:

Financial risks involve factors related to financing, leverage, and capital structure, such as mortgage debt, interest rates, loan-to-value ratios, and debt service coverage ratios. High levels of debt, variable interest rates, and inadequate cash reserves can expose investors to financial risks, such as default, foreclosure, or liquidity problems, especially during economic downturns or market downturns.

4. **Operational Risks**:

Operational risks encompass factors associated with property management, maintenance, tenant relations, and regulatory compliance. Inadequate property maintenance, tenant turnover, rent arrears, and legal disputes can disrupt cash flow, increase expenses, and affect property performance, highlighting the importance of effective property management practices and risk mitigation strategies.

5. **Legal and Regulatory Risks**:

Legal and regulatory risks arise from changes in laws, regulations, zoning ordinances, building codes, environmental regulations, and property taxes that affect real estate investments. Non-compliance with legal requirements, zoning restrictions, or environmental regulations can result in fines, penalties, litigation, and reputational damage, necessitating thorough due diligence and compliance measures.

6. **Competitive Risks**:

Competitive risks stem from competition within the real estate market, such as oversupply, new development projects, changing consumer preferences, and technological advancements. Investors must assess competitive risks, market positioning, and differentiation strategies to identify opportunities, mitigate threats, and maintain a competitive edge in the market.

7. **Rewards**:

Despite the inherent risks, real estate investments offer potential rewards and benefits, including capital appreciation, rental income, tax advantages, portfolio diversification, inflation protection, and wealth accumulation over time. By leveraging market opportunities, strategic planning, and risk management techniques, investors can maximize returns and achieve their financial goals through real estate investments.

Assessing risks and rewards in real estate investments requires a comprehensive understanding of market dynamics, property fundamentals, financial metrics, and risk factors. Investors should conduct thorough due diligence, seek professional advice, and develop investment strategies that align with their risk tolerance, investment objectives, and long-term financial goals. By carefully weighing risks against potential rewards and implementing risk mitigation strategies, investors can navigate the complexities of real estate investing and build a resilient and profitable investment portfolio over time.

3. Legal and Regulatory Factors

Legal and regulatory factors play a critical role in real estate investments, influencing property ownership, development, leasing, financing, and operations. Understanding and complying with applicable laws, regulations, and governmental requirements are essential for investors to mitigate risks, protect assets, and ensure legal compliance throughout the investment lifecycle. Several key legal and regulatory factors impact real estate investments:

a. **Zoning and Land Use Regulations**:

Zoning ordinances, land use regulations, and planning laws govern how properties can be developed, used, and modified within specific geographic areas. Investors must understand zoning classifications, setback requirements, height restrictions, and permitted land uses to assess development potential, comply with regulatory requirements, and obtain necessary approvals for property development projects.

b. **Building Codes and Construction Standards**:

Building codes, construction standards, and safety regulations establish minimum requirements for the design, construction, and maintenance of buildings and structures. Compliance with building codes, fire safety standards, accessibility requirements, and environmental regulations is essential for ensuring structural integrity, occupant safety, and legal liability protection throughout the construction process and property lifecycle.

c. **Environmental Regulations and Site Remediation**:

Environmental regulations, such as the Comprehensive Environmental Response, Compensation, and Liability Act (CERCLA) and the Resource Conservation and Recovery Act (RCRA), govern environmental protection, pollution prevention, and site remediation activities associated with real estate transactions. Investors must conduct environmental due diligence, assess potential environmental liabilities, and implement remediation measures to address contamination risks and regulatory compliance requirements.

d. **Land Titles and Property Rights**:

Land titles, property rights, and real estate ownership are governed by laws, regulations, and legal principles that establish ownership rights, title conveyance procedures, and property transfer mechanisms. Investors must verify property titles, conduct title searches, and address any encumbrances, liens, or title defects that may affect ownership rights, transferability, or marketability of real estate assets.

e. **Lease Agreements and Tenancy Laws**:

Lease agreements, tenancy laws, and landlord-tenant regulations govern the rights, obligations, and legal relationships between landlords and tenants in rental properties. Investors must draft lease agreements that comply with statutory requirements, address tenant rights, eviction procedures, security deposits, rent control ordinances, fair housing laws, and other legal considerations to protect their interests and ensure lease compliance.

f. **Taxation and Fiscal Policies**:
Taxation policies, fiscal incentives, and government programs impact real estate investments, influencing property taxation, income taxation, capital gains taxation, and tax deductions for investment properties. Investors must understand tax laws, depreciation schedules, tax credits, and tax planning strategies to optimize tax efficiency, minimize tax liabilities, and maximize after-tax returns on real estate investments.

g. **Regulatory Compliance and Disclosures**:

Regulatory compliance requirements, disclosure obligations, and reporting standards vary across jurisdictions and regulatory agencies, requiring investors to adhere to legal requirements, file necessary disclosures, and maintain accurate records. Non-compliance with regulatory obligations, such as fair housing laws, anti-discrimination laws, or securities regulations, can result in legal liabilities, fines, penalties, and reputational damage for investors.

h. **Legal Due Diligence and Risk Management**:

Legal due diligence involves conducting thorough investigations, reviewing legal documents, and identifying potential legal risks, liabilities, and contingencies associated with real estate transactions. Investors should engage legal counsel, real estate attorneys, and subject matter experts to assess legal risks, negotiate contractual terms, and implement risk management strategies to mitigate legal exposure and safeguard investments.

By addressing legal and regulatory factors proactively, investors can navigate legal complexities, mitigate compliance risks, and protect their interests in real estate investments. By staying informed, seeking professional advice, and adhering to legal requirements, investors can minimize legal uncertainties, optimize investment performance, and achieve their financial objectives in the real estate market.

1. Portfolio Allocation

Portfolio allocation within real estate involves strategically distributing investment capital across different types of properties, geographic regions, asset classes, and investment strategies to achieve diversification, minimize risks, and optimize investment returns. Effective portfolio allocation is essential for balancing risk and reward, enhancing portfolio stability, and achieving long-term investment objectives in real estate. Here are key considerations for portfolio allocation within real estate:

a. **Asset Classes**:
Real estate offers various asset classes, including residential properties, commercial properties, industrial properties, retail properties, hospitality assets, and specialized properties (such as healthcare facilities, self-storage facilities, or data centers). Investors can allocate capital across different asset classes based on

investment goals, risk tolerance, and market conditions to diversify exposure and capture opportunities in diverse real estate sectors.

b. **Property Types**:

Property types within each asset class vary in terms of risk, return potential, and market dynamics. Residential properties may include single-family homes, multifamily apartment buildings, condominiums, or student housing, while commercial properties may include office buildings, shopping centers, warehouses, or mixed-use developments. By diversifying property types within their portfolios, investors can mitigate sector-specific risks and capitalize on opportunities in different market segments.

c. **Geographic Locations**:

Geographic diversification involves investing in properties located in different cities, states, or countries to spread risk and reduce exposure to local market conditions, economic cycles, and geopolitical risks. Investors may target primary markets (such as major metropolitan areas), secondary markets (such as regional cities), or tertiary markets (such as suburban or rural areas) based on growth prospects, demand-supply dynamics, and investment preferences.

d. **Investment Strategies**:

Real estate investment strategies, such as buy-and-hold, value-add, opportunistic, or income-focused strategies, offer distinct risk-return profiles and investment objectives. Investors may allocate capital across different investment strategies to balance risk exposure, generate income, and capitalize on market opportunities at various stages of the real estate cycle.

e. **Risk Management**:

Portfolio allocation serves as a risk management tool, allowing investors to diversify risk factors, such as market risk, sector risk, concentration risk, and liquidity risk, across multiple investments. By spreading investments across diverse assets and strategies, investors can reduce portfolio volatility, mitigate downside risks, and enhance overall portfolio resilience in the face of market uncertainties.

f. Capital Allocation:

Capital allocation involves determining the optimal allocation of investment capital across different real estate assets and strategies based on return expectations, risk assessments, and portfolio objectives. Investors may allocate capital dynamically over time, rebalancing their portfolios to reflect changing market conditions, investment opportunities, and risk preferences.

g. Performance Monitoring:

Monitoring portfolio performance, tracking investment metrics, and conducting periodic reviews are essential for assessing portfolio allocation effectiveness, identifying underperforming assets, and making informed investment decisions. Investors should evaluate key performance indicators, such as total return, yield on investment, occupancy rates, cash flow, and asset appreciation, to gauge portfolio performance and adjust allocation strategies accordingly.

h. **Professional Advice**:

Seeking professional advice from real estate advisors, portfolio managers, financial planners, and investment consultants can provide valuable insights, expertise, and guidance on portfolio allocation strategies. Experienced professionals can help investors develop customized allocation plans, optimize asset allocation, and navigate market complexities to achieve their investment objectives within real estate.

By carefully allocating investment capital across diverse real estate assets, sectors, and strategies, investors can build resilient, well-balanced portfolios that mitigate risks, enhance returns, and achieve long-term financial objectives. Through strategic portfolio allocation, investors can harness the wealth-building potential of real estate investments while managing risk exposure and optimizing investment performance across market cycles.

2. Geographic Diversification

Geographic diversification is a fundamental strategy in real estate investing that involves spreading investment capital across different geographic locations to mitigate risks, capitalize on market opportunities, and enhance portfolio resilience. By investing in properties located in diverse regions, investors can reduce exposure to localized market risks, economic fluctuations, regulatory changes, and geopolitical uncertainties, thereby optimizing risk-adjusted returns and achieving long-term investment objectives. Here are key aspects of geographic diversification in real estate investing:

a. **Market Dynamics**:
Real estate markets vary significantly across different geographic regions, exhibiting distinct supply-demand dynamics, economic drivers, population trends, and market cycles. Primary markets,

such as major metropolitan areas, may offer higher liquidity, stronger growth prospects, and greater investment opportunities, while secondary and tertiary markets may provide niche opportunities, lower competition, and higher yields.

b. **Economic Indicators**:

Economic factors, such as GDP growth, employment trends, income levels, and industry diversification, influence real estate market performance and investment prospects in specific geographic regions. Investors analyze economic indicators and market fundamentals to identify regions with stable economic conditions, robust job markets, population growth, and favorable business environments conducive to real estate investment.

c. **Demographic Trends**:

Demographic trends, including population growth, migration patterns, urbanization, and aging demographics, shape real estate demand and investment opportunities in different regions. Investors target regions with growing populations, strong demographic fundamentals, and favorable demographic trends, such as millennial migration to urban centers, aging baby boomers seeking retirement destinations, or workforce expansion in emerging markets.

d. **Property Market Factors**:

Property market factors, such as rental yields, property values, affordability, housing supply, and demand-supply imbalances, vary across geographic locations and influence investment decisions. Investors assess property market dynamics, analyze local housing markets, and compare investment metrics, such as cap rates, rental growth, vacancy rates, and home prices, to identify markets with attractive risk-adjusted returns and investment potential.

e. **Regulatory Environment**:

Regulatory factors, including tax policies, land-use regulations, zoning laws, permitting processes, and landlord-tenant laws, impact real estate investment feasibility and risk exposure in different regions. Investors evaluate regulatory environments, compliance requirements, and legal frameworks to assess investment risks, mitigate regulatory uncertainties, and ensure legal compliance when investing in diverse geographic locations.

f. **Risk Mitigation**:

Geographic diversification serves as a risk management strategy, allowing investors to spread risks associated with specific regions, economic conditions, natural disasters, or geopolitical events. By diversifying across multiple markets, investors can reduce exposure to localized risks, such as economic downturns, natural hazards, regulatory changes, or supply-demand imbalances that may adversely affect property values or investment performance.

g. **Investment Objectives**:

Geographic diversification aligns with investment objectives, risk tolerance, and portfolio goals, enabling investors to achieve balanced exposure to different real estate markets and asset classes. Whether seeking income generation, capital appreciation, or portfolio stability, investors tailor geographic allocation strategies to meet specific investment objectives, optimize returns, and minimize downside risks within their investment portfolios.

h. **Portfolio Resilience**:

Geographic diversification enhances portfolio resilience and reduces volatility by spreading investments across regions with different economic drivers, market cycles, and risk profiles. A well-diversified portfolio that encompasses properties in multiple geographic locations can withstand localized market downturns, economic shocks, or unforeseen events, preserving capital, sustaining income, and maintaining long-term investment performance.

By incorporating geographic diversification into their investment strategies, real estate investors can build robust, well-balanced portfolios that mitigate risks, capture opportunities, and achieve sustainable returns over time. Through thorough market analysis, risk assessment, and strategic allocation of investment capital, investors can leverage the benefits of geographic diversification to optimize real estate investment outcomes and achieve their financial goals across diverse markets and economic environments.

3. Asset Class Diversification

Asset class diversification is a strategic approach in real estate investing that involves allocating investment capital across different types of real estate assets to optimize risk-adjusted returns, capitalize on market opportunities, and enhance portfolio resilience. By diversifying across various asset classes within the real estate sector, investors can spread risk exposure, mitigate sector-specific risks, and achieve a well-balanced investment portfolio tailored to their financial goals and risk tolerance. Here are key aspects of asset class diversification in real estate investing:

a. **Residential Properties**:
Residential properties encompass single-family homes, condominiums, townhouses, apartments, and multifamily rental properties. Investing in residential real estate offers stable rental income, long-term appreciation potential, and

diversification benefits. Residential properties cater to diverse tenant demographics, provide essential housing needs, and offer investment flexibility across different market segments and geographic locations.

b. **Commercial Properties**:

Commercial properties include office buildings, retail centers, shopping malls, industrial warehouses, and mixed-use developments. Commercial real estate offers income stability, higher rental yields, and value appreciation potential. Commercial properties serve as income-generating assets with long-term lease agreements, tenant diversification, and potential for capital growth driven by economic growth, population density, and market demand.

c. **Industrial Properties**:

Industrial properties comprise distribution centers, logistics facilities, manufacturing plants, and warehouse facilities. Investing in industrial real estate benefits from the growth of e-commerce, supply chain logistics, and global trade. Industrial properties provide stable cash flow, long-term lease agreements, and high occupancy rates driven by tenant demand for distribution, storage, and last-mile delivery services.

d. **Retail Properties**:

Retail properties include shopping centers, strip malls, freestanding retail stores, and mixed-use retail developments. Retail real estate offers income stability, diversified tenant mix, and value creation potential. Retail properties cater to consumer spending patterns, lifestyle preferences, and demographic trends, with leasing opportunities across various retail formats, brands, and market segments.

e. **Hospitality Assets**:

Hospitality assets encompass hotels, resorts, motels, and vacation rentals.

Investing in hospitality real estate offers income generation, capital appreciation, and exposure to tourism and travel trends. Hospitality properties benefit from leisure and business travel demand, destination attractions, and hospitality services, with investment opportunities in urban markets, resort destinations, and emerging tourism hubs.

f. Specialized Properties:

Specialized properties include healthcare facilities, senior housing, student housing, self-storage facilities, data centers, and niche real estate assets. Investing in specialized real estate offers niche market exposure, income diversification, and demographic-driven demand. Specialized properties serve specific needs, such as healthcare services, aging populations, student accommodations, or data storage solutions, with unique investment drivers and risk-return profiles.

g. **Mixed-Use Developments**:

Mixed-use developments combine residential, commercial, retail, and recreational components within integrated urban environments. Investing in mixed-use real estate offers income diversification, synergistic benefits, and value creation potential. Mixed-use developments cater to diverse lifestyle preferences, urbanization trends, and placemaking strategies, with investment opportunities in vibrant urban centers, transit-oriented developments, and lifestyle destinations.

h. **Portfolio Optimization**:

Asset class diversification enables investors to optimize portfolio performance, balance risk exposure, and achieve diversified income streams across real estate assets. By allocating capital strategically across different asset classes, investors can capitalize on sector-specific strengths, market opportunities, and investment cycles while mitigating risks associated with concentrated investments in a single asset class or sector.

i. **Risk Mitigation**:

Asset class diversification serves as a risk management strategy, reducing portfolio volatility and exposure to sector-specific risks, market fluctuations, and economic downturns. Diversifying across various real estate asset classes helps investors spread risk factors, such as tenant concentration, lease expirations, property types, and market dependencies, thereby enhancing portfolio resilience and minimizing downside risks.

j. **Market Opportunities**:

Asset class diversification allows investors to capitalize on diverse market opportunities, investment trends, and sector-specific growth drivers within the real estate sector. By accessing multiple asset classes, investors can identify attractive risk-adjusted returns, market niches, and investment themes aligned with changing consumer preferences, technological advancements, and industry dynamics.

By incorporating asset class diversification into their investment strategies, real estate investors can build resilient, well-balanced portfolios that optimize risk-adjusted returns, capture market opportunities, and achieve sustainable long-term investment performance across diverse real estate sectors and asset classes. Through thorough market analysis, risk assessment, and strategic allocation of investment capital, investors can leverage the benefits of asset class diversification to achieve their financial goals and objectives in the dynamic real estate market landscape.

Chapter 4

Advantages of Real Estate Investments

A. Tangible Asset Value

Real estate investments offer tangible asset value, providing investors with physical properties and land assets that have intrinsic worth and durability. Unlike financial assets such as stocks, bonds, or cryptocurrencies, which represent ownership interests or claims on future cash flows, real estate investments offer tangible assets that can be seen, touched, and utilized for various purposes. Here are some key advantages of tangible asset value in real estate investments:

1. **Preservation of Wealth**: Real estate assets serve as a store of value, preserving wealth over time through physical

ownership of land and properties. Unlike paper assets that may lose value due to market volatility or economic instability, real estate investments provide a hedge against inflation, currency depreciation, and financial market fluctuations, maintaining intrinsic value and purchasing power over the long term.

2. **Capital Appreciation**: Real estate properties have the potential to appreciate in value over time, driven by factors such as supply-demand dynamics, economic growth, and property improvements. Property appreciation allows investors to build equity, increase net worth, and achieve capital gains through property appreciation, leveraging tangible asset value to generate wealth and achieve investment objectives.

3. **Income Generation**: Real estate investments offer multiple income streams, including rental income, lease payments, and property appreciation, providing

investors with consistent cash flow and passive income. Rental properties generate rental income from tenants, while commercial properties generate lease income from tenants or occupants, enhancing cash flow and financial stability through tangible asset value and income-producing properties.

4. **Collateral for Financing**: Real estate assets serve as collateral for mortgage loans, lines of credit, and other forms of financing, allowing investors to leverage tangible asset value to access capital, expand investment portfolios, and finance property acquisitions. Lenders view real estate properties as tangible assets with intrinsic value, providing security and assurance for loans, enabling investors to utilize leverage effectively and optimize capital structure.

5. **Portfolio Diversification**: Real estate investments offer diversification benefits by complementing traditional financial assets

with tangible assets, non-correlated returns, and alternative investment opportunities. Real estate assets have low correlation with stocks, bonds, and other asset classes, providing diversification benefits, reducing overall investment risk, and enhancing portfolio resilience to market fluctuations.

6. **Tangible Utility and Use**: Real estate properties provide tangible utility and use for residential, commercial, industrial, or recreational purposes, serving as essential assets for shelter, workspace, production, and leisure activities. Real estate investments offer tangible benefits beyond financial returns, including lifestyle benefits, community amenities, and utility value for occupants, enhancing the appeal and intrinsic value of real estate assets.

7. **Tax Benefits**: Real estate investments offer various tax advantages and incentives that can enhance after-tax returns, minimize tax liabilities, and optimize investment

performance for investors. Tax benefits associated with real estate investments may include depreciation deductions, mortgage interest deductions, property tax deductions, capital gains tax deferral, and tax-free exchanges, providing investors with tax-efficient investment strategies and wealth-building opportunities.

In summary, tangible asset value is a key advantage of real estate investments, providing investors with physical properties, land assets, and income-producing assets that have intrinsic worth, durability, and utility value. By leveraging tangible asset value, investors can preserve wealth, generate income, access financing, diversify portfolios, and achieve long-term financial success through real estate investments.

B. Income Generation Potential

Real estate investments offer significant income generation potential through various revenue streams, including rental income, lease payments, and property appreciation. The income generated from real estate assets provides investors with consistent cash flow, passive income, and wealth accumulation opportunities. Here are key aspects of income generation potential in real estate investments:

1. **Rental Income**:

Rental income is one of the primary sources of income for real estate investors, derived from leasing properties to tenants in exchange for periodic rental payments. Residential, commercial, and industrial properties generate rental income based on lease agreements, occupancy rates, and rental market conditions. Rental income provides investors with a steady cash flow stream, predictable revenue, and passive income that can cover property expenses, mortgage payments, and generate surplus income for reinvestment or personal use.

2. Lease Payments:

Lease payments from commercial tenants, such as office tenants, retail tenants, and industrial tenants, contribute to income generation for real estate investors. Commercial leases typically involve long-term lease agreements, fixed or variable rent payments, and additional income streams, such as common area maintenance (CAM) charges, property taxes, insurance premiums, and tenant reimbursements. Lease payments provide investors with stable cash flow, contractual revenue, and income security over the lease term.

3. Property Appreciation:

Real estate investments offer potential for property appreciation over time, driven by market demand, economic growth, population growth, and supply-demand dynamics. Property appreciation increases the value of real estate assets, allowing investors to realize capital gains when selling properties or refinancing equity. Appreciation potential varies across different real estate markets, property types, and geographic locations, providing investors with opportunities to build wealth and increase net worth through asset appreciation.

4. **Equity Build-Up**:

Mortgage amortization and principal paydown contribute to equity build-up for real estate investors, increasing ownership stake and wealth accumulation over time. With each mortgage payment, investors reduce the outstanding loan balance and increase equity in the property. Equity build-up enhances asset value, reduces leverage, and strengthens financial position, enabling investors to leverage equity for additional investments, portfolio expansion, or wealth-building strategies.

5. **Passive Income**:

Real estate investments offer passive income opportunities, allowing investors to earn income without active involvement in day-to-day operations or management activities. Rental properties, REIT investments, and real estate partnerships provide investors with passive income streams that require minimal effort, time commitment, or expertise. Passive income from real estate investments supports financial independence, retirement planning, and lifestyle flexibility, allowing investors to diversify income sources and achieve passive wealth accumulation over time.

6. **Tax Advantages**:

Real estate investments offer various tax advantages and incentives that enhance income generation and optimize after-tax returns for investors. Tax benefits may include depreciation deductions, mortgage interest deductions, property tax deductions, capital gains tax deferral, and tax-free exchanges, allowing investors to minimize tax liabilities, preserve more of their investment gains, and increase after-tax income from real estate investments.

7. **Inflation Hedge**:

Real estate investments serve as an inflation hedge, providing protection against inflationary pressures and preserving purchasing power over time. Rental income and property values tend to increase with inflation, allowing investors to maintain real returns and wealth preservation in inflationary environments. Real assets, such as real estate, offer intrinsic value, tangible assets, and income-generating properties that retain value and provide income stability during inflationary periods.

8. **Portfolio Diversification**:

Real estate investments offer portfolio diversification benefits, complementing traditional financial assets, such as stocks and bonds, with non-correlated returns, income stability, and capital appreciation potential. By diversifying investment portfolios across different asset classes, including real estate, investors can spread risk, enhance risk-adjusted returns, and achieve balanced investment portfolios that withstand market volatility and economic uncertainties.

Real estate investments provide investors with income generation potential, passive income streams, and wealth accumulation opportunities through various revenue sources, including rental income, lease payments, property appreciation, equity build-up, and tax advantages. By leveraging income-generating properties, optimizing rental strategies, and capitalizing on market opportunities, investors can achieve financial goals, generate passive income, and build long-term wealth through real estate investments.

C. Tax Benefits

Real estate investments offer a wide range of tax benefits and incentives that can enhance after-tax returns, minimize tax liabilities, and optimize investment performance for investors. Understanding and leveraging tax advantages associated with real estate investments is essential for maximizing income, preserving wealth, and achieving long-term financial goals. Here are key tax benefits of real estate investments:

1. **Depreciation Deductions**:
Real estate investors can claim depreciation deductions on investment properties, allowing them to allocate a portion of the property's value as a non-cash expense over its useful life. Depreciation deductions reduce taxable income, lower tax liabilities, and increase cash flow by offsetting rental income with depreciation expenses. Accelerated depreciation methods, such as cost segregation studies,

enable investors to front-load depreciation deductions and maximize tax savings in the early years of property ownership.

2. **Mortgage Interest Deductions**:

Mortgage interest payments on real estate loans are tax-deductible for investment properties, providing investors with significant tax savings. Investors can deduct mortgage interest expenses from rental income, reducing taxable income and lowering overall tax liabilities. Mortgage interest deductions apply to loans used to acquire, improve, or refinance investment properties, including mortgage interest on primary residences converted into rental properties.

3. **Property Tax Deductions**:

Property taxes paid on investment properties are tax-deductible for real estate investors, allowing them to reduce taxable income and lower tax liabilities. Property tax deductions include real estate taxes levied by local governments, municipalities, and taxing authorities based on the assessed value of the property. Deductible property taxes contribute to lower operating expenses, increased cash flow, and improved after-tax returns for real estate investments.

4. Capital Gains Tax Deferral:

Real estate investments offer capital gains tax deferral opportunities through tax-deferred exchanges, such as 1031 exchanges, which allow investors to defer capital gains taxes on the sale of investment properties by reinvesting proceeds into like-kind replacement properties. 1031 exchanges enable investors to defer recognition of capital gains, preserve investment capital, and leverage tax-deferred growth for portfolio expansion or wealth-building strategies without immediate tax consequences.

5. Passive Activity Losses:

Real estate investors may offset passive activity losses from rental properties against passive income, such as rental income or income from other passive investments, to reduce taxable income and offset tax liabilities. Passive losses result from rental property expenses exceeding rental income, including depreciation, property maintenance, repairs, and operating expenses. Passive activity loss rules allow investors to deduct passive losses against passive income within certain limitations and eligibility criteria.

6. **Tax-Free Cash-Out Refinancing**:

Real estate investors can access tax-free cash through cash-out refinancing of investment properties, leveraging equity appreciation to extract capital without triggering taxable income or capital gains. Cash-out refinancing allows investors to refinance existing mortgages at favorable interest rates, increase loan amounts, and extract equity from properties while deferring tax consequences. Tax-free cash-out refinancing provides liquidity for property improvements, debt consolidation, or reinvestment without incurring immediate tax liabilities.

7. **Qualified Business Income Deduction (QBI):**

Real estate investments structured as pass-through entities, such as partnerships, LLCs, S corporations, and real estate investment trusts (REITs), may qualify for the QBI deduction under the Tax Cuts and Jobs Act (TCJA). The QBI deduction allows eligible taxpayers to deduct up to 20% of qualified business income from pass-through entities, reducing taxable income and lowering effective tax rates on real estate-related income generated through qualified business activities.

8. **Opportunity Zone Tax Benefits:**

Investing in designated Opportunity Zones provides tax incentives, including deferral, reduction, and elimination of capital gains taxes on qualified investments in economically distressed communities. Opportunity Zone investments offer tax benefits, such as temporary deferral of capital gains recognition, step-up in basis for capital gains reinvested in Opportunity Zone funds, and potential elimination of capital gains taxes on long-term investments held in Opportunity Zones for specified periods.

By leveraging tax benefits associated with real estate investments, investors can optimize after-tax returns, maximize cash flow, and enhance overall investment performance. Consulting with tax professionals, accountants, and financial advisors can help investors navigate complex tax laws, maximize tax savings, and implement tax-efficient strategies tailored to their real estate investment objectives and financial circumstances.

D. Inflation Hedge

Real estate investments serve as an effective hedge against inflation, providing investors with protection against the erosion of purchasing power and preserving wealth over time. Inflation hedge properties offer intrinsic value, tangible assets, and income-producing characteristics that can withstand inflationary pressures and generate positive real returns. Here are key ways in which real estate investments act as an inflation hedge:

1. **Appreciation Potential**:
Real estate assets have historically demonstrated appreciation potential, with property values tending to increase over time in response to inflationary pressures, market demand, and economic growth. Property appreciation allows investors to preserve and grow their wealth in real terms, as property values adjust upward in line with inflation, enabling investors to

maintain purchasing power and asset value over the long term.

2. **Rental Income Growth**:

Rental income from real estate investments tends to increase with inflation, as rental rates adjust upward over time to reflect rising living costs, wage inflation, and market demand. Real estate leases often include escalation clauses or periodic rent reviews that allow landlords to adjust rents in response to inflationary pressures, ensuring that rental income keeps pace with inflation and maintains its purchasing power over time.

3. **Tangible Asset Value**:

Real estate investments represent tangible assets with intrinsic value, providing investors with a physical hedge against inflationary risks. Unlike financial assets, such as stocks or bonds, which may lose value in inflationary environments, real estate assets offer a tangible store of value that can withstand currency depreciation and preserve wealth through periods of rising prices and economic uncertainty.

4. **Hard Asset Characteristics**:

Real estate assets possess hard asset characteristics, including land, buildings, and improvements, which have inherent value and utility regardless of monetary fluctuations or inflationary pressures. Real estate properties serve essential needs, such as shelter, commerce, and industry, making them resilient assets that retain value and generate income even in inflationary environments.

5. **Leverage Benefits**:

Real estate investors can leverage mortgage financing to amplify inflation hedging benefits and enhance investment returns. By using leverage, investors can acquire properties with a portion of their own capital while borrowing the remaining funds from lenders. As inflation erodes the real value of debt over time, investors effectively repay loans with depreciated dollars, reducing the real cost of borrowing and increasing equity appreciation potential.

6. **Inflation-Linked Investments**:

Some real estate investments, such as inflation-linked leases, index-linked bonds, or inflation-protected securities (IPS), offer direct exposure to inflationary movements, providing investors with income streams and investment returns linked to inflation indexes, consumer price indices (CPI), or other inflation measures. Inflation-linked investments provide investors with a hedge against inflationary risks, ensuring that investment returns keep pace with rising prices and maintain purchasing power over time.

7. **Portfolio Diversification**:

Real estate investments offer portfolio diversification benefits, complementing traditional financial assets with non-correlated returns, inflation hedging properties, and income stability. By diversifying investment portfolios across different asset classes, including real estate, investors can spread risk, reduce volatility, and achieve balanced portfolios that preserve wealth and generate positive real returns in inflationary environments.

8. Inflation Expectations:

Real estate investments respond to inflation expectations, with investors seeking to hedge against anticipated inflationary pressures by allocating capital to real assets, such as real estate, commodities, and inflation-protected securities. As inflation expectations rise, demand for real estate investments typically increases, driving property values higher and enhancing inflation hedging benefits for investors.

By incorporating real estate investments into their portfolios, investors can effectively hedge against inflationary risks, preserve purchasing power, and achieve long-term wealth preservation objectives. Real estate's inflation hedging properties, income-generating potential, and tangible asset characteristics make it a valuable component of diversified investment portfolios, providing investors with resilience, stability, and growth opportunities in inflationary environments.

Chapter 5

Overcoming Challenges in Real Estate Investment

A. Market Volatility

Market volatility presents a significant challenge for real estate investors, as fluctuations in economic conditions, interest rates, supply-demand dynamics, and investor sentiment can impact property values, investment returns, and portfolio performance. While market volatility is inherent in real estate investing, investors can implement strategies to mitigate risks, capitalize on opportunities, and navigate market uncertainties effectively. Here are key strategies for overcoming market volatility in real estate investment:

1. **Diversification**:

Diversifying real estate investments across different property types, geographic locations, and investment strategies can help mitigate the impact of market volatility. By spreading investment capital across diverse assets, investors can reduce concentration risk, optimize risk-adjusted returns, and achieve portfolio stability, even in volatile market conditions.

2. **Long-Term Investment Horizon**:

Adopting a long-term investment horizon allows investors to weather short-term market fluctuations and capitalize on the long-term appreciation potential of real estate assets. Real estate investments tend to perform well over extended holding periods, with property values appreciating over time despite short-term market volatility. Maintaining a disciplined investment approach and focusing on long-term objectives can help investors ride out market cycles and achieve sustainable returns.

3. Cash Flow Management:

Maintaining adequate cash reserves and liquidity buffers can help investors navigate market volatility, unexpected expenses, and income disruptions. Adequate cash flow management ensures that investors have sufficient funds to cover property expenses, mortgage payments, and operating costs during periods of market uncertainty or economic downturns, reducing financial stress and preserving investment performance.

4. Risk Assessment and Due Diligence:

Conducting thorough risk assessments and due diligence on real estate investments is essential for identifying potential risks, evaluating market conditions, and making informed investment decisions. Investors should assess property fundamentals, market trends, tenant quality, and macroeconomic indicators to gauge investment risks, anticipate market volatility, and implement risk mitigation strategies proactively.

5. **Adaptive Investment Strategies**:
Adopting adaptive investment strategies that can adjust to changing market conditions, emerging trends, and investor preferences is crucial for navigating market volatility effectively. Flexibility in investment strategies allows investors to capitalize on market opportunities, adjust portfolio allocations, and pivot investment focus in response to evolving market dynamics and economic uncertainties.

6. **Professional Advice and Expertise**:
Seeking advice from real estate professionals, financial advisors, and industry experts can provide valuable insights, market intelligence, and strategic guidance for navigating market volatility. Experienced professionals can offer expertise in market analysis, risk management, portfolio optimization, and

investment strategies tailored to individual investor goals and risk tolerance levels.

7. **Active Portfolio Management**:

Actively managing real estate portfolios, monitoring market trends, and rebalancing asset allocations can help investors adapt to changing market conditions and optimize portfolio performance. Active portfolio management involves assessing investment objectives, adjusting risk exposures, and implementing tactical investment decisions to capitalize on market opportunities and mitigate downside risks.

8. **Stress Testing and Scenario Analysis**:

Conducting stress testing and scenario analysis on real estate investments can help investors assess portfolio resilience, sensitivity to market shocks, and potential downside risks under adverse conditions. By simulating different market scenarios, investors can identify vulnerabilities, stress-test investment strategies, and implement risk mitigation measures to enhance portfolio robustness and withstand market volatility effectively.

Despite the challenges posed by market volatility, real estate investors can overcome these obstacles by adopting prudent investment strategies, maintaining a long-term perspective, and leveraging diversification, cash flow management, risk assessment, and professional expertise to navigate market uncertainties and achieve their investment objectives. Through disciplined portfolio management, proactive risk management, and adaptive investment approaches, investors can capitalize on market opportunities, mitigate downside risks, and build resilient real estate portfolios that deliver sustainable returns over time.

B. Financing Options

Financing is a critical aspect of real estate investment, providing investors with access to capital to acquire properties, fund development projects, or expand investment portfolios. Understanding the various financing options available in the real estate market is essential for investors to optimize leverage, manage liquidity, and enhance investment returns. Here are some common financing options for real estate investments:

1. Traditional Mortgages:
Traditional mortgages are a popular financing option for residential real estate investments, allowing investors to purchase properties with a down payment and repay the loan over a fixed term, typically 15 to 30 years. Mortgage loans are secured by the property itself, with the property serving as collateral for the loan. Traditional mortgages offer competitive interest rates,

predictable monthly payments, and long repayment terms, making them accessible to individual investors and homeowners.

2. **Commercial Mortgages**:

Commercial mortgages are loans used to finance commercial real estate properties, including office buildings, retail centers, industrial warehouses, and multifamily complexes. Commercial mortgages may have different terms and underwriting criteria compared to residential mortgages, with loan amounts based on property income, cash flow, and value. Commercial mortgage terms vary, ranging from short-term bridge loans to long-term permanent financing, tailored to property type, investor objectives, and market conditions.

3. **Private Lenders**:

Private lenders, including private equity firms, hedge funds, and individual investors, offer alternative financing options for real estate investors, providing capital for property acquisitions, development projects, or distressed property acquisitions. Private lenders may offer flexible terms, fast approval processes, and customized financing solutions tailored to specific investment opportunities, leveraging their network, expertise, and risk tolerance to structure deals that traditional lenders may not accommodate.

4. **Hard Money Loans**:

Hard money loans are short-term, asset-based loans secured by real estate, typically used by investors for fix-and-flip projects, distressed property acquisitions, or bridge financing. Hard money lenders focus on the property's value rather than the borrower's creditworthiness, offering fast funding, minimal documentation requirements, and higher interest rates compared to traditional loans. Hard money loans provide investors with access to quick capital for time-sensitive opportunities or situations where traditional financing is not available.

5. **Seller Financing**:

Seller financing, also known as owner financing or seller carryback financing, occurs when the property seller provides financing to the buyer instead of or in addition to a traditional mortgage. Seller financing arrangements may involve installment payments, balloon payments, or lease-to-own structures, allowing buyers to purchase properties with minimal down payments and flexible terms negotiated directly with the seller. Seller financing offers benefits for both buyers and sellers, including faster closings, reduced closing costs, and greater flexibility in deal structuring.

6. **Real Estate Crowdfunding**:

Real estate crowdfunding platforms enable investors to pool capital and invest in real estate properties or projects through online platforms. Crowdfunding platforms offer various investment opportunities, including equity investments, debt investments, and preferred equity, allowing investors to participate in real estate deals with lower capital requirements and diversify their portfolios across multiple properties or projects. Real estate crowdfunding provides access to curated investment opportunities, transparent due diligence, and passive income streams for individual investors seeking exposure to real estate assets.

7. **Government Programs and Incentives**:

Government-sponsored programs and incentives, such as FHA loans, VA loans, USDA loans, and first-time homebuyer programs, provide financing options and incentives for eligible borrowers to purchase residential properties. These programs offer favorable terms, reduced down payment requirements, and mortgage insurance options to facilitate homeownership and stimulate housing affordability. Government-backed loans and assistance programs support access to housing finance for underserved communities, low-income households, and qualified borrowers with limited financial resources.

8. **Real Estate Investment Trusts (REITs)**:

Real Estate Investment Trusts (REITs) are publicly traded companies that own, operate, or finance income-producing real estate assets, offering investors exposure to diversified real estate portfolios through stock investments. REITs provide a passive investment vehicle for investors to access real estate markets, earn dividends, and benefit from capital appreciation without direct property ownership. REITs offer liquidity, diversification, and tax advantages compared to direct real estate investments, making them a popular choice for investors seeking exposure to real estate with lower capital requirements and portfolio flexibility.

Choosing the right financing option depends on factors such as investment objectives, property type, investor profile, and market conditions. By evaluating financing options, comparing terms, and aligning financing strategies with investment goals, real estate investors can optimize capital structure, leverage financial leverage, and achieve their investment objectives effectively.

C. Regulatory Changes

Regulatory changes can significantly impact the real estate investment landscape, introducing new regulations, policies, and compliance requirements that affect property ownership, development, financing, and operations. These changes may stem from shifts in government policies, legislative reforms, zoning ordinances, environmental regulations, tax laws, or industry standards, influencing market dynamics, investment strategies, and investor behavior. Real estate investors must stay informed about regulatory developments, anticipate potential implications, and adapt their investment strategies to comply with evolving regulatory requirements. Here are key considerations for navigating regulatory changes in real estate investment:

1. **Legislative Reforms**:

Legislative reforms, including changes in real estate laws, land-use regulations, zoning codes, and building codes, can impact property development, construction standards, and investment feasibility. Investors should monitor legislative developments, engage with policymakers, and assess the implications of regulatory reforms on property values, investment returns, and project viability.

2. **Tax Policy Changes**:

Changes in tax laws, such as modifications to property tax rates, capital gains taxes, depreciation rules, and tax incentives, can affect real estate investment returns, cash flow projections, and after-tax profitability. Investors should evaluate the tax implications of regulatory changes, consult with tax advisors, and adjust investment strategies to optimize tax efficiency and minimize tax liabilities within changing regulatory environments.

3. **Environmental Regulations**:

Environmental regulations, including environmental impact assessments, remediation requirements, and sustainability standards, can influence property development, land use, and investment decisions. Investors should consider environmental risks, compliance obligations, and sustainability factors when evaluating real estate investments, particularly in environmentally sensitive areas or properties with potential environmental liabilities.

4. **Land Use Policies**:

Land use policies, urban planning initiatives, and development regulations implemented by local governments can shape property values, development opportunities, and investment prospects in specific geographic areas. Investors should assess the impact of land use policies, zoning changes, and development restrictions on property usage, density, and development potential when evaluating investment opportunities.

5. **Rent Control Measures**:

Rent control ordinances, tenant protection laws, and rental housing regulations may restrict rent increases, impose eviction restrictions, or mandate tenant rights, impacting rental income, landlord-tenant relations, and property management practices. Investors should be aware of rent control measures in target markets, assess their impact on rental yields, and factor regulatory compliance costs into investment analysis and cash flow projections.

6. **Financial Regulations**:

Financial regulations, such as lending standards, mortgage regulations, and banking policies, can affect real estate financing options, loan availability, and credit conditions for property acquisitions and development projects. Investors should stay informed about changes in financial regulations, monitor interest rate trends, and evaluate financing alternatives to optimize capital structure and funding sources for real estate investments.

7. Compliance Requirements:

Regulatory changes may introduce new compliance requirements, reporting obligations, or disclosure standards for real estate investments, requiring investors to adhere to legal and regulatory frameworks governing property ownership, leasing, and operations. Investors should maintain compliance with applicable laws, regulations, and industry standards, implement risk management protocols, and adopt best practices to ensure regulatory compliance and mitigate legal risks.

8. Risk Mitigation Strategies:

Implementing risk mitigation strategies, such as legal due diligence, regulatory compliance assessments, and contingency planning, can help investors navigate regulatory changes and mitigate potential legal, financial, or operational risks associated with real estate investments. By proactively identifying regulatory risks, investors can develop risk mitigation plans, monitor compliance obligations, and respond effectively to regulatory challenges as they arise.

Navigating regulatory changes in real estate investment requires proactive risk management, regulatory compliance, and adaptive investment strategies to adapt to evolving legal, tax, environmental, and financial regulations. By staying informed about regulatory developments, engaging with industry stakeholders, and aligning investment strategies with regulatory requirements, investors can effectively manage regulatory risks, capitalize on market opportunities, and achieve their investment objectives in a dynamic regulatory environment.

D. Property Management Issues

Effective property management is essential for maximizing returns, maintaining asset value, and ensuring tenant satisfaction in real estate investments. However, property management issues can arise, posing challenges for investors, landlords, and property managers. Addressing these issues requires proactive management strategies, efficient operations, and responsive tenant services to optimize property performance and mitigate risks. Here are common property management issues and strategies for addressing them:

1. **Tenant Turnover**:
Tenant turnover can disrupt cash flow, increase vacancy rates, and incur leasing costs for property owners. To minimize tenant turnover, property managers should focus on tenant retention strategies, such as responsive communication, timely maintenance, competitive rental rates, and

tenant amenities. Building positive relationships with tenants, addressing their needs promptly, and offering lease incentives can encourage lease renewals and reduce turnover rates.

2. **Maintenance and Repairs**:
Property maintenance and repair issues, such as deferred maintenance, aging infrastructure, and unexpected repairs, can affect property condition, tenant satisfaction, and operational efficiency. Property managers should implement proactive maintenance programs, conduct regular property inspections, and address maintenance issues promptly to prevent property deterioration, minimize repair costs, and preserve asset value. Outsourcing maintenance tasks to qualified contractors and service providers can ensure quality workmanship and timely resolution of maintenance issues.

3. **Rent Collection**:

Rent collection problems, including late payments, delinquent accounts, and tenant defaults, can impact cash flow and financial performance for property owners. Property managers should establish clear rent collection policies, communicate payment expectations to tenants, and enforce lease provisions consistently to ensure timely rent payments. Implementing automated rent collection systems, offering flexible payment options, and addressing tenant payment challenges promptly can improve rent collection efficiency and reduce arrears.

4. **Tenant Complaints and Disputes**:

Tenant complaints, disputes, and conflicts can arise from various issues, such as noise disturbances, maintenance concerns, lease disagreements, or neighbor disputes. Property managers should address tenant complaints promptly, mediate disputes effectively, and resolve conflicts amicably to maintain positive tenant relations and preserve the reputation of the property.

Open communication, conflict resolution techniques, and proactive tenant engagement can help prevent escalation of disputes and foster a harmonious living environment.

5. **Property Inspections and Compliance**:

Compliance issues, regulatory violations, and safety concerns can arise from inadequate property inspections, failure to meet building codes, or non-compliance with legal requirements. Property managers should conduct regular property inspections, identify compliance issues, and address safety hazards promptly to ensure property compliance with applicable laws, regulations, and industry standards. Implementing safety protocols, emergency preparedness plans, and risk management procedures can mitigate liability risks and maintain property compliance.

6. **Lease Administration**:

Lease administration tasks, such as lease negotiations, lease renewals, lease enforcement, and lease terminations, require efficient management and documentation to protect landlord interests and enforce lease terms. Property managers should maintain accurate lease records, monitor lease expirations, and proactively renew leases to minimize vacancies and maintain occupancy levels. Enforcing lease provisions, addressing lease violations, and documenting lease transactions can strengthen landlord-tenant relationships and protect property interests.

7. **Property Security and Risk Management**:
Property security concerns, such as theft, vandalism, trespassing, or unauthorized access, pose risks to tenant safety, property assets, and liability exposure. Property managers should implement security measures, such as access control systems, surveillance cameras, lighting

enhancements, and security patrols, to deter criminal activities and protect property assets. Conducting risk assessments, maintaining insurance coverage, and implementing risk management protocols can mitigate security risks and liability exposure for property owners.

8. **Tenant Screening and Selection**:

Tenant screening and selection processes are critical for identifying qualified tenants, minimizing rental risks, and preserving property value. Property managers should conduct comprehensive tenant screenings, including credit checks, background checks, income verification, and rental history verification, to assess tenant suitability and financial stability. Implementing rigorous tenant qualification criteria, adhering to fair housing laws, and conducting thorough applicant screenings can mitigate tenant-related risks and ensure the selection of responsible tenants.

By addressing property management issues proactively, implementing effective management practices, and prioritizing tenant satisfaction, property owners and managers can optimize property performance, minimize risks, and enhance investment returns in real estate assets. Continuous monitoring, proactive communication, and responsive action are essential for maintaining operational efficiency, preserving asset value, and achieving long-term success in property management.

E. Economic Factors

Economic factors play a significant role in shaping the performance, demand, and investment opportunities in the real estate market. Fluctuations in economic indicators, such as GDP growth, employment levels, interest rates, inflation, and consumer confidence, can influence property values, rental rates, financing costs, and investment returns. Understanding the impact of economic factors on real estate fundamentals is essential for investors to make informed decisions, assess market conditions, and navigate investment opportunities effectively. Here are key economic factors affecting the real estate market:

1. **GDP Growth**:

Economic growth, as measured by Gross Domestic Product (GDP), is a key driver of real estate demand, investment activity, and market dynamics. Strong GDP growth stimulates business expansion, job creation, and household income growth, driving demand for commercial properties, office space, retail space, and residential housing. Conversely, economic downturns or recessionary periods may lead to reduced demand, increased vacancies, and downward pressure on property values.

2. **Employment Trends**:

Employment levels and job market conditions have a direct impact on real estate demand, rental markets, and residential housing affordability. Low unemployment rates, wage growth, and job stability support household formation, rental demand, and homebuying activity, driving occupancy rates and rental growth in residential properties. Conversely, rising unemployment, job losses, or economic uncertainty may lead to decreased demand, tenant turnover, and rental affordability challenges.

3. Interest Rates:

Interest rates, as set by central banks and monetary policy decisions, influence borrowing costs, mortgage rates, and financing conditions for real estate investments. Low-interest rates stimulate real estate investment activity, incentivize property acquisitions, and increase affordability for homebuyers, driving demand for residential properties and commercial real estate assets. Conversely, rising interest rates may dampen investment appetite, increase financing costs, and reduce property affordability, impacting investment returns and property valuations.

4. Inflation:

Inflationary pressures affect real estate investment returns, property values, and purchasing power over time. Moderate inflation can enhance property values, rental income, and asset appreciation by preserving real purchasing power and increasing property demand as a hedge against currency depreciation. However, high inflation rates may erode purchasing power, reduce real returns, and increase operating costs for property owners, posing challenges for income generation and asset preservation.

5. Consumer Confidence:

Consumer confidence levels, sentiment, and spending behavior influence housing demand, retail sales, and commercial property occupancy. High consumer confidence levels indicate optimism about economic prospects, job security, and income growth, driving consumer spending, housing demand, and retail activity. Conversely, low consumer confidence may lead to cautious spending, reduced retail sales, and subdued housing demand, impacting property occupancy rates and investment performance.

6. Supply-Demand Dynamics:

Supply-demand dynamics, including housing inventory levels, construction activity, and market imbalances, influence property values, rental rates, and investment opportunities. Supply shortages, limited housing inventory, or supply chain disruptions may lead to supply constraints, housing affordability challenges, and upward pressure on property prices. Conversely, oversupply conditions, excessive construction activity, or market saturation may result in increased vacancies, rental concessions, and downward pressure on rents and property values.

7. **Demographic Trends**:

Demographic factors, such as population growth, household formation, and migration patterns, drive real estate demand, preferences, and investment trends. Population growth, urbanization, and millennial migration to urban centers fuel demand for rental housing, multifamily properties, and mixed-use developments in vibrant urban markets. Understanding demographic trends, lifestyle preferences, and generational shifts is essential for identifying emerging market opportunities and tailoring real estate investments to meet evolving consumer demand.

8. Global Economic Conditions:

Global economic conditions, geopolitical events, and international trade dynamics can impact real estate markets, investment flows, and capital markets' stability. Global economic trends, such as economic recessions, trade tensions, or currency fluctuations, may influence investor sentiment, capital allocation decisions, and cross-border investment activity in real estate assets. Monitoring global economic indicators, geopolitical risks, and international market trends is essential for assessing macroeconomic risks and opportunities in real estate investment portfolios.

By analyzing and monitoring economic factors, investors can gain insights into market trends, identify investment opportunities, and make informed decisions to optimize risk-adjusted returns and achieve their investment objectives in the dynamic real estate market environment. Economic indicators serve as valuable tools for assessing market conditions, evaluating investment risks, and positioning real estate portfolios to capitalize on market opportunities while mitigating downside risks associated with economic uncertainties and market volatility.

Chapter 6

Conclusion

A. Recap of Key Points

In conclusion, real estate investment presents significant opportunities for wealth building, income generation, and portfolio diversification, particularly as a hedge against inflation and economic volatility. Throughout this guide, we have explored various aspects of real estate investment, from understanding market fundamentals to overcoming challenges and leveraging opportunities in the dynamic real estate market environment. Here's a recap of the key points discussed:

1. **Inflation Hedge**: Real estate investments offer intrinsic value, tangible assets, and income-producing properties that serve as effective hedges against

inflation, preserving purchasing power and generating positive real returns over time.

2. **Types of Real Estate Investments**: Investors can choose from a diverse range of real estate investment options, including residential properties, commercial properties, land acquisition, REITs, and off-plan projects, each offering unique advantages and opportunities for wealth accumulation.

3. **Understanding the Real Estate Market**: An overview of the real estate sector, market dynamics, and investment strategies is essential for investors to navigate market conditions, assess investment opportunities, and optimize portfolio performance.

4. **Property Management Issues**: Effective property management practices, tenant relations, maintenance strategies, and risk management protocols are critical

for maximizing returns, mitigating risks, and maintaining property value in real estate investments.

5. **Economic Factors**: Economic indicators, such as GDP growth, employment trends, interest rates, and consumer confidence, impact real estate market dynamics, investment returns, and property performance, influencing investment decisions and market trends.

6. **Regulatory Changes**: Regulatory reforms, tax policies, environmental regulations, and compliance requirements shape real estate investment landscapes, affecting property ownership, development, financing, and operational practices, requiring investors to stay informed and adapt to changing regulatory environments.

7. **Wealth Building Strategies**: Long-term property investment, short-term flipping, rental income, and REIT

investments are effective wealth-building strategies that offer income generation, capital appreciation, and portfolio diversification benefits for investors.

8. **Risk Management and Diversification**: Diversifying real estate portfolios, conducting due diligence, managing risks, and adapting investment strategies are essential for mitigating downside risks, optimizing returns, and achieving long-term investment success in real estate.

In summary, real estate investment offers a compelling avenue for investors to build wealth, generate passive income, and achieve financial independence, provided they understand market fundamentals, adopt sound investment strategies, and navigate challenges effectively. By leveraging the insights, strategies, and best practices outlined in this guide, investors can capitalize on real estate opportunities, overcome obstacles, and achieve their investment goals in the dynamic and rewarding world of real estate investment.

B. Importance of Real Estate in Wealth Building

Real estate investment plays a crucial role in wealth building strategies due to its unique characteristics, income-generating potential, and wealth preservation benefits. Here are several reasons why real estate is essential for wealth accumulation:

1. **Tangible Asset Value**: Real estate represents tangible assets with intrinsic value, including land, buildings, and improvements, providing investors with a physical store of wealth that can withstand market volatility and economic uncertainty. Unlike financial assets, which may fluctuate in value based on market sentiment or economic conditions, real estate assets offer stability, durability, and long-term value appreciation, serving as a reliable store of wealth over time.

2. **Income Generation**: Real estate investments offer multiple income streams, including rental income, lease payments, and property appreciation, providing investors with consistent cash flow and passive income. Rental properties generate rental income from tenants, while commercial properties, such as office buildings, retail centers, and industrial warehouses, generate lease income from tenants or occupants. The steady income generated by real estate investments can supplement other sources of income, support lifestyle expenses, and provide financial security for investors.

3. **Portfolio Diversification**: Real estate investments offer diversification benefits by complementing traditional financial assets, such as stocks, bonds, and mutual funds, with non-correlated returns and alternative investment opportunities. Real estate assets have low correlation with other asset classes, meaning they may perform

differently under various market conditions, providing portfolio diversification benefits and reducing overall investment risk. Diversifying investment portfolios with real estate assets can enhance risk-adjusted returns, mitigate volatility, and improve portfolio resilience to market fluctuations.

4. **Capital Appreciation**: Real estate properties have the potential to appreciate in value over time, driven by factors such as supply-demand dynamics, economic growth, and property improvements. Property appreciation allows investors to build equity, increase net worth, and achieve capital gains through property appreciation. By investing in real estate assets with growth potential, investors can capitalize on capital appreciation opportunities and enhance long-term wealth accumulation.

5. **Inflation Hedge**: Real estate serves as an effective hedge against inflation, as property values and rental income tend to

increase in line with inflationary pressures and rising living costs. Real estate assets offer intrinsic value, tangible assets, and income-producing properties that preserve purchasing power and generate positive real returns over time. Investing in real estate allows investors to hedge against inflationary risks, protect wealth from currency depreciation, and maintain asset value in inflationary environments.

6. **Tax Benefits**: Real estate investments offer various tax advantages and incentives that can enhance after-tax returns, minimize tax liabilities, and optimize investment performance for investors. Tax benefits associated with real estate investments may include depreciation deductions, mortgage interest deductions, property tax deductions, capital gains tax deferral, and tax-free exchanges, providing investors with tax-efficient investment strategies and wealth-building opportunities.

7. **Leverage**: Real estate investments can be leveraged through mortgage financing, allowing investors to amplify returns and increase purchasing power by using borrowed funds to acquire properties. Mortgage leverage enables investors to control larger assets with a portion of their own capital, magnifying investment returns and enhancing wealth-building potential. By leveraging real estate investments, investors can achieve higher returns on equity, accelerate wealth accumulation, and expand investment portfolios.

Overall, real estate investment offers significant advantages and opportunities for wealth building, income generation, and portfolio diversification, making it a fundamental component of comprehensive wealth management strategies. By incorporating real estate assets into investment portfolios, investors can benefit from the stability, income, growth potential, and tax advantages offered by real estate investments, positioning themselves for long-term financial success and wealth accumulation.

C. Future Outlook for Real Estate Investments

The future outlook for real estate investments is influenced by a myriad of factors, including demographic trends, technological advancements, urbanization, environmental considerations, and macroeconomic conditions. While uncertainties and challenges may arise, real estate continues to be a resilient and attractive asset class for investors seeking long-term growth, income generation, and wealth preservation. Here are key trends shaping the future outlook for real estate investments:

1. **Demographic Shifts**:
Changing demographic patterns, including population growth, urbanization, and aging demographics, influence real estate demand, housing preferences, and investment opportunities. The rise of millennials as a key demographic cohort

drives demand for urban living, rental housing, and mixed-use developments, shaping investment strategies and market dynamics in vibrant urban centers. Additionally, the aging population fuels demand for senior housing, healthcare facilities, and age-restricted communities, creating opportunities for specialized real estate investments catering to the needs of older adults.

2. **Technology Disruption**:

Technological innovations, such as artificial intelligence, blockchain, smart buildings, and proptech solutions, revolutionize the real estate industry, enhancing operational efficiency, tenant experience, and asset performance. Digital transformation and data-driven analytics enable real-time monitoring, predictive maintenance, and personalized services, optimizing property management practices and enhancing investment returns. Embracing technology-driven solutions and innovation is essential for real estate investors to stay competitive, adapt to changing market trends, and capitalize on emerging opportunities in the digital era.

3. **Sustainability and ESG Investing**:
Environmental, Social, and Governance (ESG) considerations increasingly influence real estate investment decisions, driving demand for sustainable, green, and socially responsible properties. Investors prioritize energy-efficient buildings, sustainable development practices, and green building certifications to mitigate environmental risks, enhance asset value, and meet regulatory requirements. Sustainable investing strategies, such as green bonds, impact investing, and renewable energy projects, offer opportunities for investors to align financial returns with positive social and environmental outcomes, driving innovation and resilience in the real estate sector.

4. **Urbanization and Mixed-Use Development**:

Urbanization trends and the rise of mixed-use developments reshape urban landscapes, driving demand for transit-oriented developments, walkable neighborhoods, and live-work-play environments. Mixed-use projects integrate residential, commercial, retail, and recreational amenities, creating vibrant, sustainable communities that appeal to diverse demographics and lifestyle preferences. Investors capitalize on mixed-use development opportunities to diversify revenue streams, optimize land use, and enhance property value through placemaking, urban regeneration, and community-focused initiatives.

5. **Remote Work and Flexible Spaces**:

The shift towards remote work and flexible work arrangements, accelerated by the COVID-19 pandemic, influences real estate demand, office space utilization, and workplace design. Employers and tenants prioritize flexibility, collaboration, and employee well-being, driving demand for flexible office spaces, coworking facilities, and hybrid work environments. Real estate investors adapt to changing office dynamics by reimagining office layouts, enhancing technology infrastructure, and providing amenities that support remote work, collaboration, and employee productivity.

6. **Infrastructure Investment**: Infrastructure investment and public-private partnerships (PPPs) stimulate economic growth, enhance connectivity, and drive demand for real estate assets located in infrastructure-rich regions. Investments in transportation, transit systems, digital infrastructure, and sustainable infrastructure projects create development opportunities, improve accessibility, and increase property values in transit-oriented corridors and growth hubs. Real estate investors capitalize on

infrastructure-led growth by investing in properties located in strategic locations with access to transportation nodes, amenities, and infrastructure assets.

7. Globalization and Cross-Border Investment:

Globalization trends, cross-border investment flows, and international capital allocation influence real estate markets, investment activity, and asset pricing worldwide. Institutional investors, sovereign wealth funds, and global investors seek diversification, yield, and capital preservation through international real estate investments, driving cross-border transactions and global market integration. Real estate investors leverage international opportunities, diversify geographic exposure, and access growth markets through cross-border investment strategies, joint ventures, and strategic partnerships.

8. Regulatory Environment and Policy Changes:

Regulatory reforms, tax policies, and government interventions shape the regulatory environment for real estate investments, impacting market dynamics, investment returns, and investor behavior. Policy changes, such as zoning reforms, tax incentives, and economic stimulus measures, influence property development, investment incentives, and market sentiment, creating opportunities and challenges for real estate investors. Staying informed about regulatory developments, policy changes, and market trends is essential for investors to navigate regulatory risks and capitalize on emerging opportunities in the evolving real estate landscape.

In summary, the future outlook for real estate investments is characterized by dynamic market trends, technological advancements, demographic shifts, and sustainability considerations, presenting both challenges and opportunities for investors. By embracing innovation, adapting to market dynamics, and aligning investment strategies with long-term trends, real estate investors can position themselves for success, capitalize on emerging opportunities, and achieve sustainable returns in the evolving real estate investment landscape.

Chapter 7

Additional Resources

A. Recommended Books
1. "The Millionaire Real Estate Investor" by Gary Keller
2. "Rich Dad Poor Dad: What the Rich Teach Their Kids About Money That the Poor and Middle Class Do Not!" by Robert T. Kiyosaki
3. "The Book on Rental Property Investing: How to Create Wealth with Intelligent Buy and Hold Real Estate Investing" by Brandon Turner
4. "Approach To Flourishing: A Guide To Achieving Financial Greatness in the 21st Century" by King Smarty
5. "The ABCs of Real Estate Investing: The Secrets of Finding Hidden Profits Most Investors Miss" by Ken McElroy

B. Online Courses
1. **Real Estate Investing Bootcamp** - Udemy
2. **Real Estate Investment Analysis** - Coursera
3. **Introduction to Real Estate Finance and Investment** - MIT OpenCourseWare
4. **Real Estate Investment Trusts (REITs)** - Investopedia Academy
5. **Property Management Mastery** - Real Estate Express

C. Real Estate Investment Platforms
1. **Billionaire's Realtor Group (BRG)** - A real estate brokerage firm connecting investors with genuine real estate developers, ensuring due diligence on properties before market rollout. Properties purchased through BRG are free from government or other encumbrances. Access the marketplace:

http://portal.billionairerealtors.com/newvantage/regclientdirect.aspx?cid=4466163

2. **NPC** - An online marketplace for buying and selling single-family rental properties.

3. **PPBN** - A platform offering access to diversified real estate portfolios through flexible payment plans and REIT INVESTMENTS.

https://portal.peakperformerbusinessnetwork.com/?ref=310086

4. **AMW PROPERTIES** - A marketplace for investing in commercial real estate properties, including multifamily, office, retail, and industrial assets.

5. For further inquiries and assistance, you can contact Sixtus John at https://wa.me/c/2347061092227 ☎
+2347061092227

www.ingramcontent.com/pod-product-compliance
Lightning Source LLC
Chambersburg PA
CBHW052148220526
45471CB00004B/1583